Seal of the State of Rhode Island

CHRONOLOGY AND DOCUMENTARY HANDBOOK OF THE STATE OF
RHODE ISLAND

ROBERT I. VEXLER

State Editor

WILLIAM F. SWINDLER

Series Editor

1979 OCEANA PUBLICATIONS, INC./Dobbs Ferry, New York

Library of Congress Cataloging in Publication Data

Main entry under title:

Chronology and documentary handbook of the State of Rhode Island.

(Chronology and documentary handbooks of the States; 39)
    Bibliography: p.
    Includes index.
    SUMMARY: Contains a chronology of historical events from 1524 to 1977, a biographical directory of prominent citizens, and selected documents pertinent to Rhode Island history.
    1. Rhode Island—History—Chronology. 2. Rhode Island—Biography.   3. Rhode Island—History—Sources.   [1. Rhode Island—History] I. Vexler, Robert I.   II. Series.
F79.5.C45   974.5'002'02   78-26348
ISBN 0-379-16164-8

© Copyright 1979 by Oceana Publications, Inc.

All rights reserved. No part of this publication may be reproduced or transmitted in any form or by any means, electronic or mechanical, including photocopy, recording, xerography, or any information storage and retrieval system, without permission in writing from the publisher.

Manufactured in the United States of America

TABLE OF CONTENTS

INTRODUCTION	vii
CHRONOLOGY (1524-1977)	1
BIOGRAPHICAL DIRECTORY	21
PROMINENT PERSONALITIES	41
FIRST STATE CONSTITUTION	49
SELECTED DOCUMENTS	63
Roger Williams in Rhode Island - 1634	65
Rhode Island and Piracy - 1699	69
Proceedings of the General Assembly - 1723	73
Memorial from Rhode Island - 1789	75
The People's Constitution - 1841	79
The Freemen's Constitution - 1842	105
Dorr's Rebellion in Rhode Island - 1842	125
Rhode Island in 1907	133
Basic Facts	145
Map of Congressional Districts	146
SELECTED BIBLIOGRAPHY	147
NAME INDEX	149

ACKNOWLEDGMENT

Special recognition should be accorded Melvin Hecker, whose research has made a valuable contribution to this volume.

Thanks to my wife, Francine, in appreciation of her help in the preparation of this work.

Thanks also to my children, David and Melissa, without whose patience and understanding I would have been unable to devote the considerable time necessary for completing the state chronology series.

I also wish to acknowledge the scholarly research grant given to me by Pace University. This greatly eased the technical preparation of this work.

Robert I. Vexler
Pace University

INTRODUCTION

This projected series of *Chronologies and Documentary Handbooks of the States* will ultimately comprise fifty separate volumes—one for each of the states of the Union. Each volume is intended to provide a concise ready reference to basic data on the state, and to serve as a starting point for more extended study as the individual user may require. Hopefully, it will be a guidebook for a better informed citizenry - students, civic and service organizations, professional and business personnel, and others.

The editorial plan for the *Handbook* series falls into six divisions: (1) a chronology of selected events in the history of the state; (2) a short biographical directory of the principal public officials, e.g., governors, Senators and Representatives; (3) a short biographical directory of prominent personalities of the state (for most states); (4) the first state constitution; (5) the text of some representative documents illustrating main currents in the political, economic, social or cultural history of the state; and (6) a selected bibliography for those seeking further or more detailed information. Most of the data found in the present volume, in fact, have been taken from one or another of these references.

The current constitutions of all fifty states, as well as the federal Constitution, are regularly kept up to date in the definitive collection maintained by the Legislative Drafting Research of Columbia University and published by the publisher of the present series of *Handbooks*. These texts are available in most major libraries under the title, *Constitutions of the United States: National and State,* in two volumes, with a companion volume, the *Index Digest of State Constitutions.*

Finally, the complete collection of documents illustrative of the constitutional development of each state, from colonial or territorial status up to the current constitution as found in the Columbia University collection, is being prepared for publication in a multi-volume series by the present series editor. Whereas the present series of *Handbooks* is intended for a wide range of interested citizens, the series of annotated constitutional materials in the volumes of *Sources and Documents of U.S. Constitutions* is primarily for the specialist in government, history or law. This is not to suggest that the general citizenry may not profit equally from referring to these materials; rather it points up the separate purpose of the *Handbooks*, which is to guide the user of these and other sources of authoritative information with which he may systematically enrich his knowledge of this state and its place in the American Union.

William J. Swindler
*John Marshall Professor of Law
College of William and Mary
Series Editor*

Robert I. Vexler
*Associate Professor of History
Pace University
Series Associate Editor*

Hope
State Motto

CHRONOLOGY

1524   Giovanni da Verrazano explored Narragansett Bay for France.

1614   Andrian Block explored Block Island for the Dutch.

1636   June. Roger Williams established a colony on Narragansett Bay called Seekonk, now Providence, with a group of colonists from Massachusetts Bay. It was the first colony in America to grant complete religious tolerance.

1638   April. William Coddington and Anne Hutchinson, who had been driven out of Massachusetts, founded the town of Pocasset (now Portsmouth) on the island of Aquidneck.

            William Coddington became judge of Portsmouth and served until 1639.

1639   May 8. William Coddington and John Clarke founded the town of Newport, several miles south of Portsmouth. Coddington had split on various points with Mrs. Hutchinson.

            William Hutchinson became judge of Portsmouth, and William Coddington, judge of Newport. Both served until 1640.

1640   Estimated population: 300.

            March 12. Portsmouth and Newport were united.

            William Coddington became governor of Portsmouth and Newport. He served in the post until 1647.

1643   January. Samuel Gorton led a group of seceders from Providence to found Warwick.

1644   March 13. The Portsmouth-Newport General Court changed the name of the island from Aquidneck to the Isle of Rhodes or Rhode Island.

1

	March 24. Roger Williams was granted a charter for the colony.
1647	May 19. Portsmouth, Warwick, Newport and Providence were united.
	May 29-31. The Rhode Island General Assembly met in Portsmouth. They drew up a constitution which called for the separation of church and state.
	John Coggeshall became president of the colony. He served until 1649.
1649	John Smith became president of the colony. He served until 1650.
1650	Estimated population: 785.
	Nicholas Easton became president of Rhode Island. He served in the post until 1651.
1651	March. William Coddington received a separate charter for the island of Aquidneck. Roger Williams had the Council of State void the separate charter in October 1652.
	Samuel Gorton became president of the colony in which office he served until 1652.
1652	John Smith became president of Rhode Island. He served in the office until 1653.
1653	Gregory Dexter became president of Providence and Warwick. He served until 1654.
	John Sanford became president of Portsmouth and Newport. He served until 1654.
1654	Nicholas Easton served for a brief period of time as president of the colony.
	Roger Williams became president of Rhode Island and served until 1657.

1657	Benedict Arnold became president of the colony and served in the office until 1660.
1660	Estimated population: 1,539.
	October 18. Rhode Island was the first colony to proclaim the restoration of Charles II.
	William Benton became president of the colony and served until 1662.
1661	American Quakers held their first annual meeting in Rhode Island.
1662	January. Mr. Hacklett produced the first lime in America at Providence.
	Benedict Arnold again became president of the colony and served until 1666.
1663	July 18. Charles II granted a charter to Rhode Island which guaranteed religious freedom.
1666	William Benton became governor of Rhode Island. He served in the office until 1669.
1669	Benedict Arnold became governor of the colony again and served until 1672.
1670	Estimated population: 2,155.
1671	Stephen Mumford created the first Seventh Day Baptist Church at Newport.
1672	Nicholas Easton became governor of Rhode Island. He served in the office until 1674.
1674	William Coddington became governor of the colony. He served in the position until 1676.
1675	November 19. Josiah Winslow led a combined force from Massachusetts in storming the

	main fort of the Narragansetts, the site of present-day South Kingston.
1676	Walter Clarke became governor of Rhode Island. He served in the office until 1677.
1677	Benedict Arnold again became governor of the colony. He served until 1678.
1678	William Coddington again became governor of Rhode Island for a brief period.
	John Cranston became governor and served in the post until 1680.
1680	Estimated population: 3,017.
	Peleg Sanford became governor of Rhode Island. He served in the office until 1683.
1683	William Coddington, 2nd, became governor of the colony. He served until 1685.
1685	Henry Ball became governor. He served in the office until 1686.
1686	Walter Clarke served as governor during the year.
	The colony's charter was suspended. Governor Andros began to rule New England. He served in this capacity until the Revolution of 1689.
1689	John Coggeshall became acting governor. He served in this office until 1690.
1690	Estimated population: 4,224.
	Henry Ball became governor of the colony.
	John Easton became governor of Rhode Island and served in this capacity until 1695.
1695	Caleb Carr served as governor of the colony.

CHRONOLOGY

1696	Walter Clarke became governor of Rhode Island. He served in this office until 1698.
1698	Samuel Cranston became governor of the colony. He served in the position until 1727.
1700	Estimated population: 5,894
1703	June 22. Newport and Providence Counties were established. Newport, with its seat at Newport, was originally created as Rhode Island County. Its name was changed on June 16, 1729. Providence, with Providence as its county seat, was originally called Providence Plantations. Its name was also changed on June 16, 1729.
1710	Estimated population: 7,573.
1720	Estimated population: 11,680.
1727	Joseph Jencks became governor of Rhode Island. He served in the office until 1732.
1729	June 3. Washington County, with West Kingston as its seat, was established. Originally called Narragansett County, then King's Plantation and finally King's County, its name was changed on October 29, 1781. It was named after George Washington, commander of the Continental Armies and later first President of the United States.
	Rhode Island required ship captains to post ₤50 for each immigrant who came from any place other than England, Ireland, Jersey and Guernsey.
1730	Estimated population: 16,950.
1732	William Wanton became governor of Rhode Island. He served in the office until 1733.
1734	John Wanton became governor of the colony. He remained in the post until 1740.

1740	Estimated population: 25,255.
	Richard Ward became governor of Rhode Island. He served in the office until 1743.
1743	William Greene became governor of the colony. He remained in the position until 1745.
1745	Gideon Wanton became governor of Rhode Island, serving until 1746.
1746-47	February 17. Bristol County, with Bristol as its seat, was created. It was named for Bristol, England.
1746	William Greene became governor of the colony and served until 1747.
1747	Gideon Wanton again became governor of Rhode Island in which post he served until 1748.
1748	William Greene became governor again and served in the office until 1755.
1750	Estimated population: 33,266.
	June 11. Kent County was established, with East Greenwich as its seat. It was named for Kent County, England.
1755	Stephen Hopkins became governor of Rhode Island and remained in the post until 1757.
1757	William Greene again became governor of the colony. He served in the office until 1758.
1758	Stephen Hopkins became governor of Rhode Island and served until 1762.
1760	Estimated population: 45,471.
1762	Samuel Ward became governor of the colony and remained in the post until 1763.
1763	Stephen Hopkins became governor of Rhode Island and served in the office until 1765.

1764	Brown University was founded.
1765	Samuel Ward became governor again. He served in the office until 1767.
1767	Stephen Hopkins became governor of Rhode Island again. He remained in the office until 1768.
1768	Josias Lyndon became governor and served in the position until 1769.
1769	October 24. Merchants in Providence adopted a non-importation agreement.
	Joseph Wanton became governor of Rhode Island in which position he served until 1775.
1770	Estimated population: 58,196.
1772	June 9. Patriots burned the customs schooner *Gaspee*. It had run aground at Nomquit Point, seven miles from Providence.
1774	May 17. Rhode Island issued the first call for an intercolonial congress.
1775	May. Nathaniel Green was appointed commander of the Rhode Island Militia.
	Nicholas Cooke became governor of Rhode Island. He served in the office until 1778.
1776	May 4. Rhode Island's assembly declared independence from Britain.
	The British occupied Newport.
1778	August 9. Major-general John Sullivan and a French fleet led by Count D'Estaing crossed to the northern part of Rhode Island. Lord Howe and his British fleet arrived while the French were landing. Count D'Estaing brought his troops back on board the ships and went out to engage the British.

	August 20. Count D'Estaing returned to port with his fleet badly crippled.
	August 30. American troops evacuated Rhode Island.
	William Greene, 2nd, became governor of Rhode Island and served until 1786.
1779	October 25. The British left Newport.
1780	Estimated population: 52,946.
	July 11. 5,000 French soldiers and the French fleet arrived at Newport. They remained there until 1781.
1784	The assembly abolished slavery.
1786	John Collins became governor. He served until 1790.
1787	Rhode Island refused to send delegates to the United States Constitutional Convention at Philadelphia.
1788	March 24. A popular referendum rejected the United States Constitution.
1790	Population: 68,825.
	May. Arthur Fenner, Federalist and Democrat-Republican (about 1800), became governor of the state. He served in the office until his death on October 15, 1805.
	May 29. Rhode Island became the 13th state to ratify the United States Constitution by a narrow margin of 34 to 32 in its convention.
	December 21. Samuel Slater opened the first cotton mill in the United States at Pawtucket.
1794	March 31. The state legislature ratified the 11th Amendment to the United States Constitution.

1800	Population: 69,122. The legislature established the public school system, but it was abolished in 1803.
1804	February 27 and March 12. The state legislature ratified the 12th Amendment to the United States Constitution.
1805	October 15. Henry Smith, Democrat-Republican, became acting governor of the state. He served in the office until 1806.
1806	Isaac Wilbur, Democrat-Republican, became governor of the state. He served until May, 1807.
1807	May. James Fenner, Democrat-Republican, became governor of Rhode Island. He served in the office until May 1811.
1810	Population: 76,931.
1811	May. William Jones, Federalist, became governor of the state. He served in the post until May, 1817.
1817	May. Nehemiah R. Knight, Democrat-Republican, became governor of Rhode Island. He remained in the post until his resignation on January 9, 1821.
1819	The Moses Brown School was established in Providence.
1820	Population: 83,059.
1821	January 9. William C. Gibbs, Democrat Republican, became governor of the state upon the resignation of Governor Nehemiah R. Knight. Gibbs served in the office until May, 1824.
1824	May. James Fenner, Democrat-Republican (until 1826), National Republican (to 1829)

and Jackson Democrat, became governor. He served in the gubernatorial office until 1831.

The first recorded strike involving female employees occurred in Pawtucket where male and female weavers struck against a reduction in wages and an increase in hours.

1828   The public school system was reestablished.

1830   Population: 97,199.

1831   Lemuel H. Arnold, National Republican, became governor of the state. He served in the office until 1833.

1833   John B. Francis, Democrat and Anti-Masonic, became governor. He served in the post until 1838.

1838   William Sprague, Whig, became governor of Rhode Island. He remained in the office until 1839.

1839   Lieutenant Governor Samuel Ward King, Whig, became governor of the state. He served in the post until 1843.

1840   Population: 108,830.

Thomas W. Dorr began a campaign for extension of suffrage, reapportionment of representation and establishment of an independent judiciary.

1841   October 4. An unauthorized convention met at Providence to frame a constitution. It continued to meet on November 18. The delegates drafted the People's Constitution which was ratified by a large majority on December 27-29, 1841.

1842   February. The state legislature which was alarmed at the prospect of the people's rebellion drew up the Freeman's constitution that modified the charter.

CHRONOLOGY

March 21-23. The residents of Rhode Island rejected the Freeman's Constitution.

April 18. Separate elections were held. Thomas Dorr was elected governor by the People's Party, and Samuel W. King was reelected by the Freeman's Party. The State Supreme Court and President Tyler refused to recognize the People's Convention. Governor King then called out the militia to put down Dorr's rebellion.

May 18. Thomas W. Dorr's followers unsuccessfully tried to seize the state arsenal. Dorr surrendered to state authorities.

September 12. The state convention met and modified the Freeman's constitution, concluding his work on November 5, 1842.

November 21-23. A new Freeman's constitution was adopted by the citizens. It permitted more residents to vote, but only natural born United States citizens.

1843	James Fenner, Whig, again became governor of the state. He served in the office until 1845.
1844	April 26. Thomas W. Dorr was convicted of high treason. He was sentenced to life imprisonment.
1845	June. The Assembly passed an act releasing Thomas W. Dorr. He was restored to the full rights of citizenship in May 1851.
1846	Byran Diman, Whig, became governor of Rhode Island. He served in the office until 1847.
1847	Elisha Harris, Whig, became governor of the state, remaining in the position until 1849.
1849	Henry B. Anthony, Whig, became governor of Rhode Island and served until 1851.

1850   Population: 147,545.

1851   Philip Allen, Democrat, became governor of
             the state. He served in the post until his
             resignation on July 20, 1853.

1852   The State legislature passed a law restrict-
             ing the death penalty.

1852   July 20. Frances M. Dimond, Democrat, be-
             came acting governor upon the resignation of
             Governor Philip Allen. Dimond served in the
             office until 1854.

1854   William W. Hoppin, Whig, and American, be-
             came governor. He served in the office until
             1857.

1857   Elisha Dyer, Republican, became governor of
             the state. He served in the position until
             1859.

1859   Thomas A. Turner, Republican, became governor
             of Rhode Island, serving until 1860.

1860   Population: 174,620.

             William Sprague, Unionist, became governor
             of the state. He served in the office until
             his resignation on March 3, 1863.

1863   March 3. William C. Cozzens, Unionist, be-
             came acting governor upon the resignation of
             Governor William Sprague. Cozzens served in
             the office until May 1863.

             May. James Y. Smith, Unionist Republican,
             became governor of Rhode Island. He served
             in the office until 1866.

1865   February 2. The state legislature ratified
             the 13th Amendment to the United States Con-
             stitution.

1866	Ambrose E. Burnside, Republican, became governor in which position he served until 1869.
1867	February 7. The state legislator ratified the 14th Amendment to the United States Constitution.
1869	Seth Padelford, Republican, became governor of the state. He served in the office until 1873. The Board of State Charities and Corrections was established.
1870	Population: 217,353. January 18. The state legislature ratified the 15th Amendment to the United States Constitution. The state legislature abolished imprisonment for debt.
1873	Henry Howard, Republican, became governor of Rhode Island. He served in the office until 1875.
1875	Henry Lippitt, Republican, became governor of the state. He remained in office until 1877.
1877	Charles C. Van Zandt, Republican became governor of Rhode Island and served until 1880. The State School of Design was established.
1880	Population: 276,531. Alfred H. Littlefield, Republican, became governor of the state. He remained in the post until 1883.
1883	Augustus O. Bourn, Republican, became governor of the state. He served in the office until 1885.

1884	October 6. The Naval War College was founded by the Navy Department at Newport.
1885	George P. Wetmore, Republican, became governor of Rhode Island. He served in the office until 1887.
1887	John W. Davis, Democrat, became governor. He served in the office until 1888.
1888	Royal C. Taft, Republican, became governor of Rhode Island. He served in the office until 1889. The state legislature abolished property qualifications for voters. The state land grant college was founded under the Morrill Acts of 1862 and 1890 as the State College of Agriculture and Mechanic Arts.
1889	Herbert W. Ladd, Republican, became governor of the state. He served in the office until 1890.
1890	Population: 345,506. John W. Davis, Democrat, again became governor and served until 1891.
1891	Herbert W. Ladd, Republican, became governor of the state again. He served in the office until 1892.
1892	D. Russell Brown, Republican, became governor of Rhode Island. He remained in the post until 1895. Rhode Island University received its charter as Rhode Island College of Agriculture and Mechanical Arts at Kingston. It opened the same year and changed to its present name in 1951.

1895	Charles W. Lippitt, Republican, became governor of the state. He served in the office until May 25, 1897.
1897	May 25. Elisha Dyer, Republican, became governor and served until May 29, 1900.
1898	The State Normal School was reorganized in Providence.
	Population: 428,556.
1900	May 29. William Gregory, Republican, became governor of Rhode Island. He remained in the office until his death on December 16, 1901.
1901	December 16. Charles Dean Kimball, Republican, became governor of the state upon the death of Governor Gregory. Kimball served in the office until January 6, 1903.
1903	January 6. L. F. C. Garvin, who had been elected in 1902, became governor of the state. He served in the office until January 3, 1905.
1905	January 3. George H. Utter, Republican, who had been elected in 1904, became governor. He served in the office until January 1, 1907.
1907	January 1. James H. Higgins, Democrat, who had been elected in 1906, became governor of Rhode Island. He served until January 5, 1909.
1909	January 5. Aram J. Pothier, Republican, who had been elected in 1908, became governor of the state. He served until January 5, 1915.
1910	Population: 542,610.
1915	January 5. R. Livingston Beeckman, Republican, who had been elected in 1914, became

governor of the state and served until
January 4, 1921.

1920
Population: 604,397.

January 6. The state legislature ratified
the 19th Amendment to the United States
Constitution.

1921
January 4. Emery J. Sans Souci, Republican,
who had been elected in 1920, became governor.
He served in the office until January 2, 1923.

1923
January 2. William S. Flynn, Democrat, who
had been elected in 1922, became governor of
Rhode Island, serving in the office until
January 6, 1925.

1925
January 6. Aram J. Pothier, Republican,
who had been elected in 1924, became governor
of the state. He was reelected in 1926 and
served in the post until his death on February 4, 1928.

1928
February 4. Lieutenant Governor Norman S.
Case, Republican, became governor of Rhode
Island upon the death of Governor Pothier.
Case was subsequently elected in 1928 and
1930 and served in the office until January
3, 1933.

1930
Population: 687,497.

1932
April 14. The state legislature ratified
the 20th Amendment to the United States
Constitution.

1933
January 3. Theodore F. Green, Democrat, who
had been elected in 1932, became governor of
the state. He was reelected in 1934 and
served in the office until January 5, 1937.

May 8. The state legislature ratified the
21st Amendment to the United States Constitution.

CHRONOLOGY 17

1937	January 5. Robert E. Quinn, Democrat, who had been elected in 1936, became governor of Rhode Island, serving in this capacity until January 3, 1939.
1939	January 3. William H. Vanderbilt, Republican who had been elected in 1938, became governor. He served until January 7, 1941.
1940	Population: 713,346.
1941	January 7. Howard McGrath, Democrat, who had been elected in 1940, became governor. He was reelected in 1942 and 1944, serving until his resignation on October 6, 1945.
1945	October 6. Lieutenant Governor John O. Pastore, Democrat, became governor of Rhode Island upon the resignation of Governor McGrath. Pastore was subsequently elected in 1946 and 1948, serving until his resignation on December 19, 1950.
1949	August 10. J. Howard McGrath was appointed United States Attorney General by President Harry S. Truman. McGrath assumed his office as a member of the cabinet on August 24.
1950	Population: 791,896. December 19. Lieutenant Governor John S. McKiernan, Democrat, became governor of Rhode Island upon the resignation of Governor John O. Pastore. McKiernan served in the position until January 2, 1951.
1951	January 2. Dennis J. Roberts, Democrat, who had been elected in 1950, became governor of the state. He was reelected in 1952, 1954, and 1956, serving until January 6, 1959.
1955	August 20. President Dwight D. Eisenhower declared Rhode Island a major disaster area because of flooding.

1956	November 6. Residents voted for a bond issue for a bonus for veterans of the Korean War.
1959	January 6. Christopher Del Sesto, Republican, who had been elected in 1958, became governor of the state. He served in the post until January 3, 1961.
1960	Population: 859,488.
1961	January 3. John A. Wolfe, Jr., Democrat, who had been elected in 1960, became governor of Rhode Island and served in the office until January 1, 1963.
	March 22. The state legislature ratified the 23rd Amendment of the United States Constitution.
1963	January 1. John H. Chaffee, Republican, who had been elected in 1962, became governor of the state. He was reelected in 1964 and 1966, serving until January 7, 1969.
	February 14. The state legislature ratified the 24th Amendment to the United States Constitution.
1966	January 28. The state legislature ratified the 25th Amendment to the United States Constitution.
1969	January 7. Frank Licht, Democrat, who had been elected in 1968, became governor of Rhode Island. He was reelected in 1970 and served in the office until January 2, 1973.
	The Newport Bridge was completed across Narragansett Bay with a 1,600 foot suspension span.
1970	Population: 946,725.

	November 3. Residents voted for an "environmental bill of rights" amendment to the state constitution.
1971	February 26. Governor Frank Licht signed the state's first income tax into operation.
	May 27. The state legislature ratified the 26th Amendment to the United States Constitution.
1972	The state legislature ratified the Equal Rights Amendment to the United States Constitution.
1976	July 11. Queen Elizabeth II of Great Britain visited Newport as part of her six-day visit to the United States.
	October 25. Senator Robert Dole, Republican, vice presidential nominee, visited Providence.
	November 2. John Joseph Garraty, Democrat, was elected governor.
1977	January. John Joseph Garraty, Democrat, became governor of Rhode Island.

BIOGRAPHICAL DIRECTORY

The selected list of governors, United States Senators and Members of the House of Representatives for Rhode Island, 1789-1977, includes all persons listed in the Chronology for whom basic biographical data was readily available. Older biographical sources are frequently in conflict on certain individuals, and in such cases the source most commonly vited by later authorities was preferred.

ALDRICH, Nelson Wilmartin
    Republican
    b. Foster, R. I., November 6, 1841
    d. New York, N. Y., April 16, 1915
    U. S. Representative, 1879-81
    U. S. Senator, 1881-1911

ALDRICH, Richard Sture
    Republican
    b. Washington, D. C., February 29, 1884
    d. Providence, R. I., December 25, 1941
    U. S. Representative, 1923-33

ALLEN, Philip
    Tariff Democrat
    b. Providence, R. I., September 1, 1785
    d. Providence, R. I., December 16, 1865
    Governor of Rhode Island, 1851-53
    U. S. Senator, 1853-59

ANTHONY, Henry Bowen
    Republican
    b. Coventry, R. I., April 1, 1815
    d. Providence, R. I., September 2, 1884
    Governor of Rhode Island, 1850-51
    U. S. Senator, 1859-84; President pro
        tempore, 1869-73

ARNOLD, Lemuel Hastings
    Liberation Whig
    b. St. Johnsbury, Vt., January 29, 1792
    d. South Kingston, Vt., June 27, 1852
    Governor of Rhode Island, 1831-32
    U. S. Representative, 1845-47

ARNOLD, Samuel Greene
    Republican
    b. Providence, R. I., April 12, 1821
    d. Providence, R. I., February 14, 1880
    U. S. Senator, 1862-63

ARNOLD, Warren Otis
    Republican
    b. Coventry, R. I., June 3, 1839
    d. Westerly, R. I., April 1, 1910
    U.S. Representative, 1887-91, 1895-97

BALLOU, Latimer Whipple
  Republican
  b. Cumberland, R. I., March 1, 1812
  d. Woonsocket, R. I., May 9, 1900
  U. S. Representative, 1875-81

BEECKMAN, R. Livingston
  Republican
  b. New York, N. Y., April 15, 1866
  d. January 21, 1935
  Governor of Rhode Island, 1915-21

BOSS, John Linscom, Jr.
  ----
  b. Charleston, S. C., September 7, 1780
  d. Newport, R. I., August 1, 1819
  U. S. Representative, 1815-19

BOURN, Augustus Osborn
  Republican
  b. Providence, R. I., October 1, 1834
  d. January 28, 1925
  Governor of Rhode Island, 1883-85

BOURN, Benjamin
  Federalist
  b. Bristol, R. I., September 9, 1755
  d. Bristol, R. I., September 17, 1808
  U. S. Representative, 1790-96

BRADFORD, William
  ----
  b. Plymouth, Mass., November 4, 1729
  d. Bristol, R. I., July 6, 1808
  U. S. Senator, 1793-97; President pro
     tempore, 1797

BRAYTON, William Daniel
  Republican
  b. Warwick, R. I., November 6, 1815
  d. Providence, R. I., June 30, 1887
  U. S. Representative, 1857-61

BROWN, Daniel Russell
  Republican
  b. Bolton, Conn., March 28, 1848
  d. February 28, 1919
  Governor of Rhode Island, 1892-95

BROWN, John
  Federalist
  b. Providence, R. I., January 27, 1736
  d. Providence, R. I., September 20, 1803

U. S. Representative, 1799-1801

BROWNE, George Huntington
Democrat
b. Gloucester, R. I., January 6, 1811
d. Providence, R. I., September 26, 1885
U. S. Representative, 1861-63

BULL, Melville
Republican
b. Newport, R. I., September 19, 1854
d. Middletown, R. I., July 5, 1909
U. S. Representative, 1895-1903

BURDICK, Clark
Republican
b. Newport, R. I., January 13, 1868
d. Newport, R. I., August 27, 1948
U. S. Representative, 1919-33

BURGES, Tristam
----
b. Rochester, Mass., February 26, 1770
d. at his estate "Watchemoket Farm" (now part of East Providence), R. I., October 13, 1853
U. S. Representative, 1825-35

BURNSIDE, Ambrose Everett
Republican
b. Liberty, Ind., May 23, 1824
d. Bristol, R. I., September 13, 1881
Governor of Rhode Island, 1866-68
U. S. Senator, 1875-81

BURRILL, James, Jr.
----
b. Providence, R. I., April 25, 1772
d. Washington, D. C., December 25, 1820
U. S. Senator, 1817-20

CAPRON, Adin Ballou
Republican
b. Mendon, Mass., January 9, 1841
d. Stillwater, R. I., March 17, 1911
U. S. Representative, 1897-1911

CASE, Norman S.
Republican
Governor of Rhode Island, 1928-33

CHACE, Jonathan
Republican

    b. Fall River, Mass., July 22, 1829
    d. Providence, R. I., June 30, 1917
    U. S. Representative, 1881-85
    U. S. Senator, 1885-89

CHAFFEE, John Hubbard
    Republican
    b. Providence, R. I., October 22, 1922
    Governor of Rhode Island, 1963-69
    U. S. Secretary of the Navy, 1969-72

CHAMPLIN, Christopher Grant
    ----
    b. Newport, R. I., April 12, 1768
    d. Newport, R. I., March 18, 1840
    U. S. Representative, 1797-1801
    U. S. Senator, 1809-11

CLARKE, John Hopkins
    Whig
    b. Elizabeth, N. J., April 1, 1789
    d. Providence, R. I., November 23, 1870
    U. S. Senator, 1847-53

COLT, LeBaron Bradford
    Republican
    b. Dedham, Mass., June 25, 1846
    d. Bristol, R. I., August 18, 1924
    U. S. Senator, 1919-24

CONDON, Francis Bernard
    Democrat
    b. Central, R. I., November 11, 1891
    d. Boston, Mass., November 23, 1965
    U. S. Representative, 1930-35

COZZENS, William C.
    Governor of Rhode Island, 1863

CRANSTON, Henry Young
    Whig
    b. Newport, R. I., October 9, 1789
    d. Newport, R. I., February 12, 1864
    U. S. Representative, 1843-47

CRANSTON, Robert Bennie
    Law and Order Whig
    b. Newport, R. I., January 14, 1791
    d. Newport, R. I., January 27, 1873
    U. S. Representative, 1837-43 (Whig),
        1847-49 (Law and Order Whig)

DAVIS, John William
    Democrat
    b. Rheoboth, Mass., March 7, 1826
    d. 1907
    Governor of Rhode Island, 1887-88, 1890-91

DAVIS, Thomas
    Democrat
    b. Dublin, Ireland, December 18, 1806
    d. Providence, R. I., July 26, 1895
    U. S. Representative, 1853-55

DEL SESTO, Christopher
    Republican
    b. Providence, R. I., March 10, 1907
    Governor of Rhode Island, 1959-61

DE WOLF, James
    Democrat
    b. Bristol, R. I., March 18, 1764
    d. New York, N. Y., December 31, 1837
    U. S. Senator, 1821-25

DIMAN, Byron
    Law and Order Whig
    Governor of Rhode Island, 1846-47

DIMOND, Francis M.
    Democrat
    Governor of Rhode Island, 1853-54

DIXON, Nathan Fellows
    Whig
    b. Plainfield, Conn., December 13, 1774
    d. Washington, D. C., January 29, 1842
    U. S. Senator, 1839-42

DIXON, Nathan Fellows (son of the preceding)
    Republican
    b. Westerly, R. I., May 1, 1812
    d. Westerly, R. I., April 11, 1881
    U. S. Representative, 1849-51 (Whig), 1863-71 (Republican)

DIXON, Nathan Fellows (son of the preceding)
    b. Westerly, R. I., August 28, 1847
    d. Westerly, R. I., November 8, 1897
    U. S. Representative, 1885
    U. S. Senator, 1889-95

DURFEE, Job
    Democrat

b. Tiverton, R. I., September 20, 1790
d. Tiverton, R. I., July 26, 1847
U. S. Representative, 1821-23 (People's Party), 1823-25 (Democrat)

DYER, Elisha
Republican
Governor of Rhode Island, 1857-59

DYER, Elisha
Republican
b. Providence, R. I., November 28, 1839
d. 1906
Governor of Rhode Island, 1897-1900

EAMES, Benjamin Tucker
Republican
b. Dedham, Mass., June 4, 1818
d. East Greenwich, R. I., October 6, 1901
U. S. Representative, 1871-79

EDDY, Samuel
Democrat
b. Johnston, near Providence, R. I., March 31, 1769
d. Providence, R. I., February 3, 1839
U. S. Representative, 1819-25

ELLERY, Christopher
Democrat
b. Newport, R. I., November 1, 1768
d. Newport, R. I., December 2, 1840
U. S. Senator, 1801-05

FENNER, Arthur
Democrat-Republican
b. Providence, R. I., December 10, 1745
d. Providence, R. I., October 15, 1805
Governor of Rhode Island, 1790-1805

FENNER, James
Democrat
b. Providence. R. I., January 22, 1771
d. on his estate "What Cheer," near Providence, R. I., April 17, 1846
U. S. Senator, 1805-07
Governor of Rhode Island, 1807-11, 1824-31, 1843-45

FLYNN, William Smith
Democrat
b. Providence, R. I., August 14, 1885

d. April 6, 1966
Governor of Rhode Island, 1923-25

FOGARTY, John Edward
    Democrat
    b. Providence, R. I., March 23, 1913
    d. Washington, D. C., January 10, 1967
    U. S. Representative, 1941-44, 1945-67

FORAND, Aime Joseph
    Democrat
    b. Fall River, Mass., May 23, 1895
    U. S. Representative, 1937-39, 1941-61

FOSTER, Theodore
    Law and Order
    b. Brookfield, Mass., April 29, 1752
    d. Providence, R. I., January 13, 1828

FRANCIS, John Brown
    Law and Order
    b. Philadelphia, Pa., May 31, 1791
    d. "Spring Green," Warwick, R. I.,
        August 9, 1864
    Governor of Rhode Island, 1833-38
    U. S. Senator, 1844-45

GARVIN, Lucius Fayette Clark
    Democrat
    b. Knoxville, Tenn., November 13, 1841
    d. October 2, 1922
    Governor of Rhode Island, 1903-05

GERRY, Peter Goelet
    Democrat
    b. New York, N. Y., September 18, 1879
    d. Providence, R. I., October 31, 1957
    U. S. Representative, 1913-15
    U. S. Senator, 1917-29, 1935-47

GRANGER, Daniel Larned Davis
    Democrat
    b. Providence, R. I., May 30, 1852
    d. Washington, D. C., February 14, 1909
    U. S. Representative, 1903-09

GREEN, Theodore Francis
    Democrat
    b. Providence, R. I., October 2, 1867
    d. Providence, R. I., May 19, 1966
    Governor of Rhode Island, 1933-36
    U. S. Senator, 1937-61

GREENE, Albert Collins
    Whig
    b. East Greenwich, R. I., April 15, 1791
    d. Providence, R. I., January 8, 1863
    U. S. Senator, 1845-51

GREENE, Ray
    ----
    b. Warwick, R. I., February 2, 1765
    d. Warwick, R. I., January 11, 1829

GREGORY, William
    Republican
    b. Astoria, N. Y., August 3, 1849
    d. 1901
    Governor of Rhode Island, 1900-01

HARRIS, Elishu
    Whig
    Governor of Rhode Island, 1847-49

HAZARD, Nathaniel
    Democrat
    b. Newport, R. I., 1776
    d. Washington, D. C., December 17, 1820
    U. S. Representative, 1819-20

HEBERT, Felix
    Republican
    b. near Hyacinthe, Province of Quebec,
        Canada, December 11, 1874
    d. Warwick, R. I., December 14, 1969
    U. S. Senator, 1929-35

HIGGINS, James Henry
    Democrat
    b. Lincoln, R. I., January 22, 1876
    d. September 16, 1927
    Governor of Rhode Island, 1907-09

HOPPIN, William Warner
    Whig, Republican
    b. Providence, R. I., September 1, 1807
    d. Providence, R. I., April 19, 1890
    Governor of Rhode Island, 1854-57

HOWARD, Henry
    Republican
    b. Cranston, R. I., April 2, 1826
    d. 1905
    Governor of Rhode Island, 1873-75

HOWELL, Jeremiah Brown
    Federalist
    b. Providence, R. I., August 28, 1771
    d. Providence, R. I., February 5, 1822
    U. S. Senator, 1811-17

HOWLAND, Benjamin
    Democrat
    b. Tiverton, R. I., July 27, 1755
    d. Tiverton, R. I., May 1, 1821
    U. S. Senator, 1804-09

HUNTER, William
    Federalist
    b. Newport, R. I., November 26, 1774
    d. Newport, R. I., December 3, 1849
    U. S. Senator, 1811-21

JACKSON, Charles
    Liberal Whig
    Governor of Rhode Island, 1845-46

JACKSON, Richard, Jr.
    Federalist
    b. Providence, R. I., July 3, 1764
    d. Providence, R. I., April 18, 1838
    U. S. Representative, 1808-15

JENCKES, Thomas Allen
    Republican
    b. Cumberland, R. I., November 2, 1818
    d. Cumberland, R. I., November 4, 1875
    U. S. Representative, 1863-71

JONES, William
    Federalist
    Governor of Rhode Island, 1811-17

KENNEDY, Ambrose
    Republican
    b. Blackstone, Mass., December 1, 1875
    d. Woonsocket, R. I., March 11, 1967
    U. S. Representative, 1913-23

KIMBALL, Charles Dean
    Republican
    b. Providence, R. I., September 13, 1859
    d. December 8, 1930
    Governor of Rhode Island, 1901-03

KING, George Gordon
    Whig
    b. Newport, R. I., June 9, 1807
    d. Newport, R. I., June 17, 1870
    U. S. Representative, 1849-53

KING, Samuel Ward
    Whig
    Governor of Rhode Island, 1840-43

KNIGHT, Nehemiah
    Anti Federalist
    b. "Knightsville," Cranston, now part of
        Providence), R. I., March 23, 1746
    d. Cranston, R. I., June 13, 1808
    U. S. Representative, 1803-08

KNIGHT, Nehemiah Rice
    Democrat
    b. Cranston, R. I., December 31, 1780
    d. Providence, R. I., April 18, 1854
    Governor of Rhode Island, 1817-21 (Anti
        Federalist)
    U. S. Senator, 1821-25 (Anti Federalist),
        1835-41 (Democrat)

LADD, Herbert Warren
    Republican
    b. New Bedford, Mass., October 15, 1843
    d. ----
    Governor of Rhode Island, 1889-90, 1891-
        92

LAPHAM, Oscar
    Democrat
    b. Burrillville, R. I., June 29, 1837
    d. Providence, R. I., March 29, 1926
    U. S. Representative, 1891-95

LEAHY, Edward Laurence
    Democrat
    b. Bristol, R. I., February 9, 1886
    d. Bristol, R. I., July 22, 1953
    U. S. Senator, 1949-50

LICHT, Frank
    Democrat
    b. Providence, R. I., March 3, 1916
    Governor of Rhode Island, 1969-73

LIPPITT, Charles Warren
    Republican
    b. Providence, R. I., July 19, 1812

d. 1902
Governor of Rhode Island, 1895-97

LIPPITT, Henry
　　Republican
　　Governor of Rhode Island, 1875-77

LIPPITT, Henry Frederick
　　Republican
　　b. Providence, R. I., October 12, 1856
　　d. Providence, R. I., December 28, 1933
　　U. S. Senator, 1911-17

MALBONE, Francis
　　Federalist
　　b. Newport, R. I., March 20, 1759
　　d. Washington, D. C., June 4, 1809
　　U. S. Representative, 1793-97
　　U. S. Senator, 1809

MASON, James Brown
　　Federalist
　　b. Thompson, Conn., January 1775
　　d. Providence, R. I., August 31, 1819
　　U. S. Representative, 1815-19

MATHEWSON, Elisha
　　Democrat
　　b. Scituate, R. I., April 18, 1767
　　d. Scituate, R. I., October 14, 1853
　　U. S. Senator, 1807-11

MCGRATH, James Howard
　　Democrat
　　b. Woonsocket, R. I., November 28, 1903
　　d. Narragansett, R. I., September 2, 1966
　　U. S. Senator, 1947-49
　　Chairman Democrat National Committee,
　　　　1947-49

MCKIERNAN, John Sammon
　　Democrat
　　b. Providence, R. I., October 15, 1911
　　Governor of Rhode Island, 1950-51

METCALF, Jesse Houghton
　　Republican
　　b. Providence, R. I., November 16, 1860
　　d. Providence, R. I., October 9, 1942
　　U. S. Senator, 1924-37

MONAST, Louis
　　Republican

b. Marieville de Moniar, Iberville, Pro-
      vince of Quebec, Canada, July 1, 1863
   d. Pawtucket, R. I., April 16, 1936
   U. S. Representative, 1927-29

NOEL, Phillip William
   Democrat
   b. Providence, R. I., May 3, 1909
   Governor of Rhode Island, 1973-

NOTTE, John Anthony, Jr.
   Democrat
   b. Providence, R. I., May 3, 1909
   Governor of Rhode Island, 1961-63

O'Connell, Jeremiah Edward
   Democrat
   b. Wakefield, Mass., July 8, 1883
   d. Cranston, R. I., September 18, 1964
   U. S. Representative, 1923-27, 1929-
      30

O'CONNELL, John Matthew
   Democrat
   b. Westerly, R. I., August 10, 1872
   d. Westerly, R. I., December 6, 1941
   U. S. Representative, 1933-39

O'SHAUNESSY, George Francis
   Democrat
   b. Galway, Ireland, May 1, 1868
   d. Providence, R. I., November 18, 1934
   U. S. Representative, 1911-19

PADELFORD, Seth
   Republican
   Governor of Rhode Island, 1869-73

PAGE, Charles Harrison
   Democrat
   b. Gloucester, R. I., July 19, 1843
   d. Providence, R. I., July 21, 1912
   U. S. Representative, 1887, 1891-93,
      1893-95

PASTORE, John Orlando
   Democrat
   b. Providence, R. I., March 17, 1907
   Governor of Rhode Island, 1945-50
   U. S. Senator, 1950-

PEARCE, Dutce Jerauld
   Democrat

b. Island of Prudence, R. I., April 3,
    1789
d. Newport, R. I., May 9, 1849
U. S. Representative, 1825-37

PELL, Claiborne de Borda
    Democrat
    b. New York, N. Y., November 22, 1918
    U. S. Senator, 1961-

PENDLETON, James Monroe
    Republican
    b. North Stonington, Conn., January 10,
        1822
    d. Westerly, R. I., February 16, 1889
    U. S. Representative, 1871-73

PIRCE, William Almy
    Republican
    b. Hope, R. I., February 29, 1824
    d. Johnston, R. I., March 5, 1891
    U. S. Representative, 1885-87

POTTER, Elisha Reynolds
    Federalist
    b. Little Rest (now Kingston), R. I.,
        November 5, 1764
    d. South Kingston, R. I., September 26,
        1835
    U. S. Representative, 1796-97, 1809-15

POTTER, Elisha Reynolds (son of the preceding)
    Whig
    b. Little Rest (now Kingston), R. I., June
        20, 1811
    d. Kingston, R. I., April 10, 1882
    U. S. Representative, 1843-45

POTTER, Samuel John
    ----
    b. South Kingston Township, R. I., June
        29, 1753
    d. Washington, D. C., October 14, 1804
    U. S. Senator, 1803-04

QUINN, Robert Emmett
    Democrat
    b. Phoenix, R. I., April 2, 1894
    d. May 19, 1975
    Governor of Rhode Island, 1937-39

RISK, Charles Francis
    Republican
    b. Central Falls, R. I., August 19, 1897
    d. Saylesville, in the township of Lincoln,
        R. I., December 26, 1943
    U. S. Representative, 1935-37, 1939-41

ROBBINS, Asher
    Whig
    b. Wethersfield, Conn., October 26, 1757
    d. Newport, R. I., February 25, 1845
    U. S. Senator, 1825-39

ROBERTS, Dennis Joseph
    Democrat
    b. Providence, R. I., April 8, 1903
    Governor of Rhode Island, 1951-59

ROBINSON, Christopher
    American Party
    b. Providence, R. I., May 15, 1806
    d. Woonsocket, R. I., October 3, 1889
    U. S. Representative, 1859-61

ST. GERMAIN, Fernand Joseph
    Democrat
    b. Blackstone, Mass., January 9, 1928
    U. S. Representative, 1961-

SANDAGER, Henry
    Republican
    b. Providence, R. I., April 12, 1887
    d. Cranston, R. I., December 24, 1955
    U. S. Representative, 1939-41

SAN SOUCI, Emery John
    Republican
    b. Saco, Maine, July 24, 1857
    d. August 19, 1936
    Governor of Rhode Island, 1921-23

SHEFFIELD, William Paine
    Republican
    b. New Shoreham, Block Island, R. I.,
    d. Newport, R. I., June 2, 1907
    U. S. Representative, 1861-63
    U. S. Senator, 1884-85

SHEFFIELD, William Paine (son of the preceding)
    Republican
    b. Newport, R. I., June 1, 1857
    d. Exeter, R. I., October 19, 1919

U. S. Representative, 1909-11

SIMMONS, James Fowler
    Whig
    b. on a farm near Little Compton, R. I.,
        September 10, 1795
    d. Johnston, R. I., July 10, 1864
    U. S. Senator, 1841-47, 1857-62

SMITH, Henry
    Democrat-Republican
    Governor of Rhode Island, 1805-06

SMITH, James Yorung
    Unionist-Republican
    b. Poquonoc Village, Groton, Conn., September 15, 1809
    d. Providence, R. I., March 26, 1876
    Governor of Rhode Island, 1863-66

SPOONER, Henry Joshua
    Republican
    b. Providence, R. I., August 6, 1839
    d. Providence, R. I., February 9, 1918
    U. S. Representative, 1881-91

SPRAGUE, William
    Whig
    b. Cranston, R. I., November 3, 1799
    d. Providence, R. I., October 19, 1856
    U. S. Representative, 1835-37
    Governor of Rhode Island, 1838-39
    U. S. Senator, 1842-44

SPRAGUE, William (nephew of the preceding)
    Republican
    b. Cranston, R. I., September 12, 1830
    d. Paris, France, September 11, 1915
    Governor of Rhode Island, 1860-63 (Unionist)
    U. S. Senator, 1863-75

STANTON, Joseph, Jr.
    Democrat
    b. Charlestown, R. I., July 19, 1739
    d. Charlestown, R. I., 1807
    U. S. Senator, 1790-93
    U. S. Representative, 1801-07

STINESS, Walter Russell
    Republican
    b. Smithfield, R. I., March 13, 1854
    d. Warwick, R. I., March 17, 1924

U. S. Representative, 1915-23

TAFT, Royal Chapin
    Republican
    b. Northbridge, Mass., February 14, 1823
    d. 1902
    Governor of Rhode Island, 1888-89

THURSTON, Benjamin Babcock
    Democrat
    b. Hopkinton, R. I., June 29, 1804
    d. New London, Conn., May 17, 1886
    U. S. Representative, 1847-49, 1851-57

TIERNAN, Robert Owens
    Democrat
    b. Providence, R. I., February 24, 1929
    U. S. Representative, 1967-

TILLINGHAST, Joseph Leonard
    Whig
    b. Taunton, Mass., 1791
    d. Providence, R. I., December 30, 1844
    U. S. Representative, 1837-43

TILLINGHAST, Thomas
    ----
    b. East Greenwich, R. I., August 21, 1742
    d. East Greenwich, R. I., August 26, 1821

TURNER, Thomas G.
    Governor of Rhode Island, 1859-60

UTTER, George Herbert
    Republican
    b. Plainfield, N. J., July 24, 1854
    d. Westerly, R. I., November 3, 1912
    Governor of Rhode Island, 1905-06
    U. S. Representative, 1911-12

VANDERBILT, William Henry
    Republican
    b. New York, N. Y., November 24, 1901
    Governor of Rhode Island, 1939-41

VAN ZANDT, Charles
    Republican and Temperance
    Governor of Rhode Island, 1877-80

WETMORE, George Peabody
    Republican
    b. London, England, August 2, 1846
    d. Boston, Mass., September 11, 1921

Governor of Rhode Island, 1885-86
U. S. Senator, 1895-1907, 1908-13

WILBOUR, Isaac
    Federalist
    b. Little Compton, R. I., April 25, 1763
    d. Little Compton, R. I., October 4, 1837
    U. S. Representative, 1807-09

WILBUR, Isaac
    Democrat-Republican
    Governor of Rhode Island, 1806-07

PROMINENT PERSONALITIES

The following select list of prominent persons of Rhode Island has been selected to indicate the valuable contributions they have made to American life.

PROMINENT PERSONALITIES

ALLEN, Zachariah
    b. September 15, 1795
    d. March 17, 1882
    Constructed first centarl furnace system for
        heating houses by hot air, 1821
    Member Town Council of Providence, 1822
    Inventor, automatic steam-engine cutoff

ANGELL, James B.
    b. Scituate, R. I., January 7, 1829
    d. April 1, 1916
    President, University of Vermont, 1860-66
    President, University of Michigan, 1871-1909
    U. S. Minister to China, 1880-81
    Author: <u>Progress in International Law</u>, 1875
        <u>Reminiscences of James B. Angell</u>, 1912

BALL, William Tillinghast
    b. Newport, R. I., May 18, 1849
    d. 1909
    Known for skill in abdominal operations
        and treatment of hernia and cancer,
        one of first American surgeons to adopt
        antisepsis

BARTLETT, John Russell
    b. Providence, R. I., October 23, 1805
    d. May 28, 1886
    Secretary of State, Rhode Island, 1855-72
    Author: <u>Dictionary of Americanisms</u>, 1848
        <u>Records of the Colony of Rhode
    Island, 1636-1792</u>, 10 vols.

BOSS, Lewis
    b. Providence, R. I., October 26, 1846
    d. October 5, 1912
    Director, Dudley Observatory and Professor
        of Astronomy, Union University, 1876-1912
    Author: <u>Declinations of Fixed Stars</u>, 1878

BROWN, John Carter
    b. Providence, R. I., August 28, 1797
    d. June 10, 1874
    Collected book collection, emphasizing
        Western Hemisphere from its discovery to
        1800 - eventually contributed to Brown
        University

BROWN, John Rogers
    b. Warren, R. I., January 26, 1810
    d. July 23, 1876

Built linear dividing engine, 1850
Perfected Bernier Caliper reading to
    thousandths of an inch, 1851
Incorporated Brown and Sharpe Manufacturing
    Co., 1868
Issued patent on Universal Grinding machine,
    1877 - after his death

BROWN, Moses
    b. Providence, R. I., September 23, 1738
    d. September 7, 1836
    Organized Rhode Island Abolition Society,
        1774
    Treasurer Friends' School, 1784
    Member Rhode Island General Assembly, 1764-71
    Founder: Providence Athenaeum Library
             Rhode Island Bible Society
             Rhode Island Peace Society

BROWN, Nicholas
    b. Providence, R. I., August 8, 1729
    d. May 29, 1791
    Constructed cannon for Revolutionary War
    Supplied clothing and munitions to American
        Army

CHANNING, Walter
    b. Newport, R. I., April 15, 1786
    d. July 27, 1876
    Professor Harvard Medical School, 1815-54
    Dean Harvard Medical School, 1819-47
    Introduced use of ether to lessen pain of
        labor

CHANNING, William Ellery
    b. Newport, R. I., April 7, 1780
    d. October 2, 1842
    Pastor, Federal Street Church, Boston,
        1803-42
    Organizer of American Unitarian Association,
        1803-42
    Author: <u>Negro Slavery</u>, 1835
            <u>Self Culture</u>, 1838
            <u>Duty of the Free States</u>, 1842

CODDINGTON, William
    b. 1601
    d. November 1, 1678
    Protested prosecution of Anne Hutchinson, 1637
    Withdrew from Massachusetts to Aquidneck,
        R. I., 1638
    Founder of Newport, R. I., 1639
    Governor of Aquidneck, 1640

PROMINENT PERSONALITIES   45

      Governor of Rhode Island and Providence
         Plantations, 1674, 1675, 1678

CORLISS, George Henry
    b. Easton, N. Y., June 2, 1817
    d. February 21, 1888
    Inventor and manufacturer of Corliss Engine, first
       steam engine to use rotary valves
    Merged John Barstow and E. J. Nightingale Co.
       into Corliss, Nightingale and Co., 1849
    Became president of Corliss Engine Co., 1856
    Member Rhode Island legislature, 1868-70

DORR, Thomas Wilson
    b. Providence, R. I., November 5, 1805
    d. December 27, 1854
    Organizer and leader, People's Party
    Leader, Dorr's Rebellion, 1844 - arrested, tried
       and convicted - sentenced to life
       imprisonment - released 1845 under act
       of general amnesty

ELLERY, William
    b. Newport, R. I., December 22, 1727
    d. February 15, 1820
    One of original incorporators of Rhode
       Island College, 1774
    Member Continental Congress, 1776-81, 1783-
       85
    Signer of Declaration of Independence, 1776
    Chief Justice of Rhode Island, 1785

GORHAM, Jabez
    b. Providence, R. I., February 18, 1792
    d. March 27, 1829
    Silversmith - first to use machinery
    Formed firm which was origin of Gorham
       Manufacturing Co., 1842
    Member Rhode Island General Assembly

GREENE, Francis Vinton
    d. Providence, R. I., June 27, 1850
    d. May 15, 1921
    Graduate U. S. Military Academy, 1870
    Military Attaché, U. S. Legation, St.
       Petersburg, 1877-79
    Professor, Practical Military Engineering,
    U. S. Military Academy, 1885-86
    New York Police Commissioner, 1903-04
    Author: <u>The Russian Army and Its Campaigns
       in Turkey</u>, 1879, 2 vols.
          <u>Army Life in Russia</u>, 1881
          <u>Our First Year in the Great War</u>, 1918

GREENE, Nathaniel
    b. Warwick, R. I., August 7, 1742
    d. June 19, 1786
    Brigadier General, Continental Army, 1775
    Supreme Commander, Continental Army during
        Washington's absence, September 1780
    Commander, Army of the South, 1780

KING, Clarence
    b. Newport, R. I., January 6, 1842
    d. 1901
    Suggested and organized U. S. Geological
    Survey - Director, 1878-81

PERRY, Matthew Galbraith
    b. Newport, R. I., April 10, 1794
    d. New York, N. Y., March 4, 1858
    Selected to negotiate treaty with Japan, 1852
    Treaty of Peace, Amity and Commerce, signed
        between United States and Japan, 1854
    Author: <u>Narrative of the Expedition of an
        American Squadron to the China Seas and
        Japan</u>, 1856

PERRY, Oliver Hazard
    b. South Kingston, R. I., August 20, 1785
    d. Angostura, Venezuela, August 23, 1819
    Supervised construction of American fleet
        on Lake Erie - defeated British in
        battle, September 9, 1813

HOPKINS, Stephen
    b. Providence, R. I., March 7, 1707
    d. Providence, R. I., April 13, 1785
    Governor of Rhode Island, 1755-57, 1758-62,
        1763-65, 1767-68
    First Chancellor, Rhode Island College (now
        Brown University), 1764
    Member Continental Congress, 1774-76, 1778
    Signer United States Declaration of Inde-
        pendence, 1776

LA FARGE, Oliver
    b. New York, N. Y., December 19, 1901
    d. August 2, 1963
    Author: <u>Laughing Boy</u>, (Pulitzer Prize for
        best novel of the year), 1929
            <u>All the Young Men</u>, 1935
            <u>War Below Zero</u>, 1944
            <u>A Pictorial History of the American
        Indian</u>, 1956

PROMINENT PERSONALITIES

MUNRO, Dana Carleton
    b. Bristol, R. I., June 7, 1866
    d. January 13, 1933
    Professor of Medieval History, Princeton University, 1915-33
    Author: The Middle Ages, 1902
    Editor. L. J. Paetow, A Guide to the Study of Medieval History, 1931

SLATER, Samuel
    b. Derbyshire, England, June 9, 1768
    d. Webster, Mass., April 21, 1835
    Established factory, Pawtucket, R. I., to reproduce cotton machinery - under firm name of Almy, Brown and Slater, 1793
    Regarded as founder of American cotton industry

WATERHOUSE, Benjamin
    b. Newport, R. I., March 4, 1754
    d. Cambridge, Mass., October 2, 1846
    First Professor of Theory and Practice of Physics, Harvard University, 1783-1812
    Known as pioneer in vaccination in America, 1800

WILCOX, Stephen
    b. Westerly, R. I., February 12, 1830
    d. Brooklyn, N. Y., November 27, 1893
    Invented safety water-tube boiler with inclined tubes - patented, 1856
    Invented generator of similar type - patented, 1867
    Organized Babcock, Wilcox and Company to manufacture his boilers and steam engines, 1867

FIRST STATE CONSTITUTION

CHARTER OF RHODE ISLAND AND PROVIDENCE PLANTATIONS— 1663 *[a]

CHARLES THE SECOND, by the grace of *God*, King of England, Scotland, France and Ireland, Defender of the Faith, &c., to all to whome these presents shall come, greeting: *Whereas wee* have been informed, by the humble petition of our trustie and well beloved subject, John Clarke, on the behalf of Benjamine Arnold, William Brenton, William Codington, Nicholas Easton, William Boulston, John Porter, John Smith, Samuell Gorton, John Weeks, Roger Williams, Thomas Olnie, Gregorie Dexter, John Cogeshall, Joseph Clarke, Randall Holden, John Greene, John Roome, Samuell Wildbore, William Ffield, James Barker, Richard Tew, Thomas Harris, and William Dyre, and the rest of the purchasers and ffree inhabitants of our island, called *Rhode-Island*, and the rest of the colonie of Providence Plantations, in the Narragansett Bay, in New-England, in America, that they, pursueing, with peaceable and loyall mindes, their sober, serious and religious intentions, of godlie edifieing themselves, and one another, in the holie Christian ffaith and worshipp as they were perswaded; together with the gaineing over and conversione of the poore ignorant Indian natives, in those partes of America,

---

* The Charter in "The Manual with Rules and orders for the use of the General Assembly of the State of Rhode Island. 1889–'90. Prepared in accordance with a Resolution of the General Assembly by Samuel H. Cross, Sec'y of State. 1889." pp. 49–64.

[a] The commonwealth of England had claimed the right, in 1651, to appoint a governor for Rhode Island and Providence Plantations, with a provincial council, to be elected by the freeholders and accepted by himself. After the restoration an agent was sent to England, who obtained this charter from Charles II.

to the sincere professione and obedienc of the same ffaith and worship, did, not onlie by the consent and good encouragement of our royall progenitors, transport themselves out of this kingdome of England into America, but alsoe, since their arrivall there, after their first settlement amongst other our subjects in those parts, ffor the avoideing of discorde, and those manie evills which were likely to ensue upon some of those oure subjects not beinge able to beare, in these remote parties, theire different apprehensiones in religious concernements, and in pursueance of the afforesayd ends, did once againe leave theire desireable stationes and habitationes, and with excessive labour and travell, hazard and charge, did transplant themselves into the middest of the Indian natives, who, as wee are infformed, are the most potent princes and people of all that country; where, by the good Providence of God, from whome the Plantations have taken their name, upon theire labour and industrie, they have not onlie byn preserved to admiration, but have increased and prospered, and are seized and possessed, by purchase and consent of the said natives, to their ffull content, of such lands, islands, rivers, harbours and roades, as are verie convenient, both for plantationes and alsoe for buildinge of shipps, suplye of pypestaves, and other merchandize; and which lyes verie commodious, in manie respects, for commerce, and to accommodate oure southern plantationes, and may much advance the trade of this oure realme, and greatlie enlarge the territories thereof; they haveinge, by neare neighbourhoode to and friendlie societie with the greate bodie of the Narragansett Indians, given them encouragement, of theire owne accorde, to subject themselves, theire people and landes, unto us; whereby, as is hoped, there may, in due tyme, by the blessing of God upon theire endeavours, bee layd a sure ffoundation of happinesse to all America:

And whereas, in theire humble addresse, they have ffreely declared, that it is much on their hearts (if they may be permitted), to hold forth a livlie experiment, that a most flourishing civill state may stand and best bee maintained, and that among our English subjects, with a full libertie in religious concernements; and that true pietye rightly grounded upon gospell principles, will give the best and greatest security to sovereignetye, and will lay in the hearts of men the strongest obligations to true loyaltye: *Now know yee*, that wee beinge willinge to encourage the hopefull undertakeinge of oure sayd loyall and loveinge subjects, and to secure them in the free exercise and enjoyment of all theire civill and religious rights, appertaining to them, as our loveing subjects; and to preserve unto them that libertye, in the true Christian ffaith and worshipp of God, which they have sought with soe much travaill, and with peaceable myndes, and loyall subjectione to our royall progenitors and ourselves, to enjoye; and because some of the people and inhabitants of the same colonie cannot, in theire private opinions, conforms to the publique exercise of religion, according to the litturgy, formes and ceremonyes of the Church of England, or take or subscribe the oaths and articles made and established in that behalfe; and for that the same, by reason of the remote distances of those places, will (as wee hope) bee noe breach of the unitie and unifformitie established in this nation: Have therefore thought ffit, and doe hereby publish, graunt, ordeyne and declare,

That our royall will and pleasure is, that noe person within the sayd colonye, at any tyme hereafter, shall bee any wise molested, punished, disquieted, or called in question, for any differences in opinione in matters of religion, and doe not actually disturb the civill peace of our sayd colony; but that all and everye person and persons may, from tyme to tyme, and at all tymes hereafter, freelye and fullye have and enjoye his and theire owne judgments and consciences, in matters of religious concernments, throughout the tract of lande hereafter mentioned: they behaving themselves peaceablie and quietlie, and not useing this libertie to lycentiousnesse and profanenesse, nor to the civill injurye or outward disturbeance of others; any lawe, statute, or clause, therein contayned, or to bee contayned, usage or custome of this realme, to the contrary hereof, in any wise, notwithstanding. And that they may bee in the better capacity to defend themselves, in theire just rights and libertyes against all the enemies of the Christian ffaith, and others, in all respects, wee have further thought fit, and at the humble petition of the persons aforesayd are gratiously pleased to declare, That they shall have and enjoye the benefitt of our late act of indempnity and ffree pardon, as the rest of our subjects in other our dominions and territoryes have; and to create and make them a bodye politique or corporate, with the powers and priviledges hereinafter mentioned.

And accordingely our will and pleasure is, and of our especiall grace, certaine knowledge, and meere motion, *wee have ordeyned*, constituted and declared, and by these presents, for us, our heires and successors, doe ordeyne, constitute and declare, That they, the sayd William Brenton, William Codington, Nicholas Easton, Benedict Arnold, William Boulston, John Porter, Samuell Gorton, John Smith, John Weekes, Roger Williams, Thomas Olneye, Gregorie Dexter, John Cogeshall, Joseph Clarke, Randall Holden, John Greene, John Roome, William Dyre, Samuell Wildbore, Richard Tew, William Ffeild, Thomas Harris, James Barker, ——— Rainsborrow, ——— Williams, and John Nickson, and all such others as now are, or hereafter shall bee admitted and made ffree of the company and societie of our collonie of Providence Plantations, in the Narragansett Bay, in New England, shall bee, from tyme to tyme, and forever hereafter, a bodie corporate and politique, in ffact and name, by the name of *The Governor and Company of the English Colony of Rhode-Island and Providence Plantations, in New-England, in America;* and that, by the same name, they and their successors shall and may have perpetuall succession, and shall and may bee persons able and capable, in the lawe, to sue and bee sued, to pleade and be impleaded, to answeare and bee answeared unto, to defend and to be defended, in all and singular suites, causes, quarrels, matters, actions and thinges, of what kind or nature soever; and alsoe to have, take, possesse, acquire and purchase lands, tenements or hereditaments, or any goods or chattels, and the same to lease, graunt, demise, aliene, bargaine, sell and dispose of, at their owne will and pleasure, as other our liege people of this our realme of England, or anie corporation or bodie politique within the same, may be lawfully doe: *And further*, that they the sayd Governor and Company, and theire successors, shall and may, forever hereafter, have a common seale, to serve and use for all matters, causes, thinges and affaires, whatsoever, of them and their successors; and the same seale to alter, change, breake, and make new, from tyme to tyme, at their will and pleasure, as they shall thinke ffitt.

And further, wee will and ordeyne, and by these presents, for us, oure heires and successours, doe declare and apoynt that, for the better ordering and managing of the affaires and business of the sayd Company, and theire successours, there shall bee one Governour, one Deputie-Governour and ten Assistants, to bee from tyme to tyme, constituted, elected and chosen, out of the freemen of the sayd Company, for the tyme beinge, in such manner and fforme as is hereafter in these presents expressed; which sayd officers shall aplye themselves to take care for the best disposeinge and orderinge of the generall businesse and affaires of, and concerninge the landes and hereditaments hereinafter mentioned, to be graunted, and the plantation thereof, and the government of the people there.. And for the better execution of oure royall pleasure herein, wee doe, for us, oure heires and successours, assign, name, constitute and apoynt the aforesayd Benedict Arnold to bee the first and present Governor of the sayd Company, and the sayd William Brenton, to bee the Deputy-Governor, and the sayd William Boulston, John Porter, Roger Williams, Thomas Olnie, John Smith, John Greene, John Cogeshall, James Barker, William Ffeild, and Joseph Clarke, to bee the tenn present Assistants of the sayd Companye, to continue in the sayd severall offices, respectively, untill the first Wednesday which shall bee in the month of May now next comeing. *And further*, wee will, and by these presents, for us, our heires and successessours, doe ordeyne and graunt, that the Governor of the sayd Company, for the tyme being, or, in his absence, by occasion of sicknesse, or otherwise, by his leave and permission, the Deputy-Governor, ffor the tyme being, shall and may, ffrom tyme to tyme, upon all occasions, give order ffor the assemblinge of the sayd Company and callinge them together, to consult and advise of the businesse and affaires of the sayd Company.

And that forever hereafter, twice in every year, that is to say, on every first Wednesday in the month of May, and on every last Wednesday in October, or oftener, in case it shall bee requisite, the Assistants, and such of the ffreemen of the Company, not exceedinge six persons ffor Newport, ffoure persons ffor each of the respective townes of Providence, Portsmouth and Warwicke, and two persons for each other place, towne or city, whoe shall bee, from tyme to tyme, thereunto elected or deputed by the majour parte of the ffreemen of the respective townes or places ffor which they shall bee so elected or deputed, shall have a generall meetinge, or Assembly then and there to consult, advise and determine, in and about the affaires and businesse of the said Company and Plantations. *And further*, wee doe, of our especiall grace, certayne knowledge, and meere motion, give and graunt unto the sayd Governour and Company of the English Colonie of *Rhode-Island and Providence Plantations*, in New-England, in America, and theire successours, that the Governour, or, in his absence, or, by his permission, the Deputy-Governour of the sayd Company, for the tyme beinge, the Assistants, and such of the ffreemen of the sayd Company as shall bee soe as aforesayd elected or deputed, or soe many of them as shall bee present att such meetinge or assemblye, as afforesayde, shall bee called the Generall

Assemblye; and that they, or the greatest parte of them present, whereof the Governour or Deputy-Governour, and sixe of the Assistants, at least to bee seven, shall have, and have hereby given and graunted unto them, ffull power authority, ffrom tyme tyme, and at all tymes hereafter, to apoynt, alter and change, such dayes, tymes and places of meetinge and Generall Assemblye, as theye shall thinke flitt; and to choose, nominate, and apoynt, such and soe manye other persons as they shall thinke flitt, and shall be willing to accept the same, to bee ffree of the sayd Company and body politique, and them into the same to admitt; and to elect and constitute such offices and officers, and to graunt such needfull commissions, as they shall thinke flitt and requisite, ffor the ordering, managing and dispatching of the affaires of the sayd Governour and Company, and their successours; and from tyme to tyme, to make, ordeyne, constitute or repeal, such lawes, statutes, orders and ordinances, fformes and ceremonies of government and magistracye as to them shall seeme meete for the good nad wellfare of the sayd Company, and ffor the government and ordering of the landes and hereditaments, hereinafter mentioned to be graunted, and of the people that doe, or att any tyme hereafter shall, inhabitt or bee within the same; soe as such lawes, ordinances and constitutiones, soe made, bee not contrary and repugnant unto, butt, as neare as may bee, agreeable to the lawes of this our realme of England, considering the nature and constitutione of the place and people there; and alsoe to apoynt, order and direct, erect and settle, such places and courts of jurisdiction, ffor the heareinge and determininge of all actions, cases, matters and things, happening within the sayd collonie and plantatione, and which shall be in dispute, and depending there, as they shall thinke flit; and alsoe to distinguish and sett forth the severall names and titles, duties, powers and limitts, of each court, office and officer, superior and inferior; and alsoe to contrive and apoynt such formes of oaths and attestations, not repugnant, but, as neare as may bee, agreeable, as aforesayd, to the lawes and statutes of this oure realme, as are conveniente and requisite, with respect to the due administration of justice, and due execution and discharge of all offices and places of trust by the persons that shall bee therein concerned; and alsoe to regulate and order the waye and manner of all elections to offices and places of trust, and to prescribe, limitt and distinguish the numbers and boundes of all places, townes or cityes, within the limitts and bounds herein after mentioned, and not herein particularlie named, who have, and shall have, the power of electing and sending of ffreemen to the sayd Generall Assembly; and alsoe to order, direct and authorize the imposing of lawfull and reasonable ffynes, mulcts, imprisonments, and executing other punishments pecuniary and corporal, upon offenders and delinquents, according to the course of other corporations within this oure kingdom of England; and agayne to alter, revoke, annull or pardon, under their common seale or otherwyse, such ffynes, mulcts, imprisonments, sentences, judgments and condemnations, as shall bee thought flitt; and to direct, rule, order and dispose of, all other matters and things, and particularly that which relates to the makinge of purchases of the native Indians, as to them shall seeme meete; whereby oure sayd people and inhabitants, in the sayd Plantationes, may be soe religiously, peaceably and civilly governed, as that, by theire good life and orderlie conversatione, they may win and invite the native Indians of the countrie to the knowledge and obedience of the onlie true God, and Saviour of mankinde; willing, commanding and requireing, and by these presents, for us, oure heires and successours, ordeyneing and apoynting, that all such lawes, statutes, orders and ordinances, instructions, impositions and directiones, as shall bee soe made by the Governour, deputye-Governour, Assistants and ffreemen, or such number of them as aforesayd, and published in writinge, under theire common seale, shall bee carefully and duely observed, kept, performed and putt in execution, accordinge to the true intent and meaning of the same.

And these our letters patent, or the duplicate or exempliffication thereof, shall bee to all and everie such officer, superiour or inferiour, ffrom tyme to tyme, for the putting of the same orders, lawes, statutes, ordinances, instructions and directions, in due execution, against us, oure heires and successours, a sufficient warrant and discharge. *And ffurther*, our will and pleasure is, and wee doe hereby, for us, oure heires and successours, establish and ordeyne, that yearelie, once in the yeare, forever hereafter, namely, the aforesayd Wednesday in May, and at the towne of Newport, or elsewhere, if urgent occasion doe require, the Governour, Deputy-Governour and Assistants of the sayd Company, and other officers of the sayd Company, or such of them as the Generall Assemblye shall thinke ffitt, shall bee, in the sayd Generall Court or Assembly to bee held from that daye or tyme, newely chosen for the year ensueing, by such greater part of the sayd Company, for the tyme beinge, as shall bee then and there present; and if itt shall happen that the present Governour, Deputy-Governour and Assistants, by these presents apoynted, or any such as shall hereafter be newly chosen into their roomes, or any of them, or any other the officers of the sayd Company, shall die or bee removed ffrom his or their severall offices or places, before the sayd generall day of election, (whom wee doe hereby declare, for any misdemeanour or default, to be removeable by the Governour, Assistants and Company, or such greater parte of them, in any of the sayd publique courts, to bee assembled as aforesayd), that then, and in every such case, it shall and may bee lawfull to and ffor the sayd Governour, Deputy-Governour, Assistants and Company aforesayde, or such greater parte of them, soe to bee assembled as is aforesayde, in any theire assemblyes, to proceede to a new election of one or more of their Company, in the roome or place, roomes or places, of such officer or officers, soe dyeinge or removed, according to theire discretiones; and immediately upon and after such electione or elections made of such Governour, Deputy-Governour or Assistants, or any other officer of the sayd Company, in manner and forme aforesayde, the authoritie, office and power, before given to the fformer Governour, Deputy-Governour, and other officer and officers, soe removed, in whose steade and place new shall be chosen, shall, as to him and them, and every of them, respectively, cease and determine:

Provided, allwayes, and our will and pleasure is, that as well such as are by these presents apoynted to bee the present Governour, Deputy-Governour and Assistants, of the sayd Company, as those that shall succeede them, and all other officers to bee apoynted and chosen as aforesayde, shall, before the undertakeinge the execution of the sayd offices and places respectively, give theire solemn engagement, by oath, or otherwyse, for the due and faythfull performance of theire duties in their severall offices and places, before such person or persons as are by these presents hereafter apoynted to take and receive the same, that is to say: the sayd Benedict Arnold, whoe is hereinbefore nominated and apoynted the present Governour of the sayd Company, shall give the aforesayd engagement before William Brenton, or any two of the sayd Assistants of the sayd Company; unto whome, *wee doe* by these presentes give ffull power and authority to require and receive the same; and the sayd William Brenton, whoe is hereby before nominated and apoynted the present Deputy-Governour of the sayd Company, shall give the aforesayed engagement before the sayd Benedict Arnold, or any two of the Assistants of the sayd Company; unto whome *wee doe* by these presents give ffull power and authority to require and receive the same; and the sayd William Boulston, John Porter, Roger Williams, Thomas Olneye, John Smith, John Greene, John Cogeshall, James Barker, William Ffeild, and Joseph Clarke, whoe are hereinbefore nominated apoynted the present Assistants of the sayd Company, shall give the sayd engagement to theire offices and places respectively belongeing, before the sayd Benedict Arnold and William Brenton, or one of them; to whome, respectively *wee doe* hereby give ffull power and authority to require, administer or receive the same: *and ffurther,* our will and pleasure is, that all and every other future Governour or Deputy-Governour, to bee elected and chosen by vertue of these presents, shall give the sayd engagement before two or more of the sayd Assistants of the sayd Company ffor the tyme beinge; unto whome wee doe by these presents give ffull power and authority to require, administer or receive the same; and the sayd Assistants, and every of them, and all and every other officer or officers to bee hereafter elected and chosen by vertue of these presents, from tyme to tyme, shall give the like engagements, to their offices and places respectively belonging bofere the Governour or Deputy-Governour for the tyme being; unto which sayd Governour, or Deputy-Governour, *wee doe* by these presents give full power and authority to require, administer or receive the same accordingly.

And wee doe likewise, for vs, oure heires and successours, give and graunt vnto the sayd Governour and Company and theire successours by these presents, that, for the more peaceable and orderly government of the sayd Plantations, it shall and may bee lawfull ffor the Governour, Deputy-Governor, Assistants, and all other officers and ministers of the sayd Company, in the administration of justice, and exercise of government, in the sayd Plantations, to vse, exercise, and putt in execution, such methods, rules, orders and directions, not being contrary or repugnant to the laws and statutes of this oure realme, as have byn heretofore given, vsed and accustomed; in such cases respectively, to be putt in practice, untill att the next or some other Generall Assembly, special provision shall be made and ordeyned in the cases aforesayd. *And wee doe ffurther,* for vs, oure heires and successours, give and graunt vnto the sayd Governour and Company, and theire successours, by these presents, that itt shall and may bee lawfull to and for the sayd Governour, or in his absence, the Deputy-Governour, and majour parte of the sayd Assistants, for the tyme being, att any tyme when the sayd Generall Assembly is not sitting, to nominate, apoynt and constitute, such and soe many commanders, governours, and military officers, as to them shall seeme requisite, for the leading, conductinge and trayneing vpp the inhabitants of the sayd Plantations in martiall affaires, and for the defence and safeguard of the sayd Plantations; and that itt shall and may bee lawfull to and for all and every such commander, governour and military officer, that shall bee soe as aforesayd, or by the Governour, or, in his absence, the Deputy-Governour, and six of the sayd Assistants, and majour parte of the ffreemen of the sayd Company present att any Generall Assemblies, nominated, apoynted and constituted accordinge to the tenor of his and theire respective commissions and directions, to assemble, exercise in arms, martiall array, and putt in warlyke posture, the inhabitants of the sayd collonie, ffor theire speciall defence and safety; and to lead and conduct the sayd inhabitants, and to encounter, expulse, expell and resist, by force of armes, as well by sea as by lande; and alsoe to kill, slay and destroy, by all fitting wayes, enterprizes and meanes, whatsoever, all and every such person or persons as shall, att any tyme hereafter, attempt or enterprize the destruction, invasion, detriment or annoyance of the sayd inhabitants or Plantations; and to vse and exercise the lawe martiall in such cases only as occasion shall necessarily require; and to take or surprise, by all wayes and meanes whatsoever, all and every such person and persons, with theire shipp or shipps, armor, ammunition or other goods of such persons, as shall, in hostile manner, invade or attempt the defeating of the sayd Plantations, or the hurt of the sayd Company and inhabitants; and vpon just causes, to invade and destroy the native Indians, or other enemyes of the sayd Collony. Neverthelesse, our will and pleasure is, and wee doe hereby declare to the rest of oure Collonies in New England, that itt shall not bee lawefull ffor this our sayd Collony of Rhode-Island and Providence Plantations, in America, in New-England, to invade the natives inhabiting within the boundes and limitts of theire sayd Collonies without the knowledge and consent of the sayd other Collonies. And itt is hereby declared, that itt shall not bee lawfull to or ffor the rest of the Collonies to invade or molest the native Indians, or any other inhabitants, inhabiting within the bounds and lymitts hereafter mentioned (they having subjected themselves vnto vs, and being by vs taken into our speciall protection), without the knowledge and consent of the Governour and Company of our Collony of Rhode-Island and Providence Plantations.

Alsoe our will and pleasure is, and wee doe hereby declare unto all Christian Kings, Princes and States, that if any person, which shall hereafter bee of the sayd Company or Plantations, or any other, by apoyntment of the sayd Governour and Company for the tyme beinge, shall at any tyme or tymes hereafter, rob or spoyle, by sea or land, or do any hurt, unlawfull hostility to any of the subjects of vs, oure heires or successours, or any of the subjects of any Prince or State, beinge then in league with vs, oure heires, or successours, vpon complaint of such injury done to any such Prince or State, or theire subjects, wee, our heires and successours, will make open proclamation within any parts of oure realme of England, ffitt ffor that purpose, that the person or persons committing any such robbery or spoyle shall, within the tyme lymitted by such proclamation, make full restitution or satisfaction of all such injuries, done or committed, soe as the sayd Prince, or others soe complaineinge, may bee fully satisfyed and contented; and if the sayd person or persons whoe shall committ any such robbery or spoyle shall not make satysfaction, accordingly, within such tyme, soe to bee lymitted, that then wee, oure heires and successours, will putt such person or persons out of oure allegiance and protection; and that then itt shall and may bee lawefull and ffree ffor all Princes or others to prosecute, with hostillity, such offenders, and every of them, theire and every of theire procurers, ayders, abettors and counsellors, in that behalfe; *Provided* alsoe, and oure expresse will and pleasure is, *and wee doe*, by these presents, ffor vs, our heirs and successours, ordeyne and apoynt, that these presents shall not, in any manner, hinder any of oure lovinge subjects, whatsoever, ffrom vseing and exercising the trade of ffishing vpon the coast of New-England, in America; butt that they, and every or any of them, shall have ffull and ffree power and liberty to continue and vse the trade of ffishing vpon the sayd coast, in any of the seas thereunto adjoyninge, or any armes of the seas, or salt water, rivers and creeks, where they have been accustomed to ffish; and to build and to sett upon the waste land, belonginge to the sayd Collony and Plantations, such wharfes, stages and worke-houses as shall be necessary for the salting, drying and keepeing of theire ffish, to be taken or gotten upon that coast. *And ffurther*, for the encouragement of the inhabitants of our sayd Collony of Providence Plantations to sett vpon the businesse of takeing whales, itt shall bee lawefull ffor them, or any of them, having struck whale, dubertus, or other greate ffish, itt or them, to pursue unto any parte of that coaste, and into any bay, river, cove, creeke or shoare, belonging thereto, and itt or them, vpon sayd coaste, or in the sayd bay, river, cove, creeke or shoare, belonging thereto, to kill and order for the best advantage, without molestation, they makeing noe wilfull waste or spoyle, any thinge in these presents conteyned, or any other matter or thing, to the contrary notwithstanding. And further alsoe, wee are gratiously pleased, and doe hereby declare, that if any of the inhabitants of oure sayd Collony doe sett upon the plantinge of vineyards (the soyle and clymate both seemeing naturally to concurr to the production of wynes), or bee industrious in the discovery of ffishing banks, in or about the sayd Collony, wee will, ffrom tyme to tyme, give and allow all due and fitting encouragement therein, as to others in cases of lyke nature. And further, of oure more ample grace, certayne knowledge, and meere motion, wee have given and graunted, and by these presents, ffor vs, oure heires and successours, doe give and graunt vnto the sayd Governour and Company of the English Collony of Rhode-Island and Providence Plantations, in the Narragansett Bay, in New-England in America, and to every inhabitant there, and to every person and persons trading thither, and to every such person or persons as are or shall bee ffree of the sayd Collony, full power and authority, from tyme to tyme, and att all tymes hereafter, to take, shipp, transport and carry away, out of any of our realmes and dominions, for and towards the plantation and defence of the sayd Collony, such and soe many of oure loveing subjects and strangers as shall or will willingly accompany them in and to their sayd Collony and Plantation; except such person or persons as are or shall be therein restrained by vs, oure heires and successours, or any law or statute of this realme: and also to shipp and transport all and all manner of goods, chattels, merchandizes, and other things whatsoever, that are or shall bee vsefull or necessary ffor the sayd Plantations, and defence thereof, and vsually transported, and nott prohibited by any lawe or statute of this our realme; yielding and paying vnto vs, our heires and successours, such the duties, customes and subsidies, as are or ought to bee payd or payable for the same.

And ffurther, our will and pleasure is, and wee doe, ffor us, our heires and successours, ordeyn, declare and graunt, vnto the sayd Governour and Company, and their successours, that all and every the subjects of vs, our heires and successours, which are already planted and settled within our sayd Collony of Providence Plantations, or which shall hereafter goe to inhabit within the sayd Collony, and all and every of theire children, which have byn borne there, or which shall happen hereafter to bee borne there, or on the sea, goeing thither, or retourneing from thence, shall have and enjoye all libertyes and immunityes of ffree and naturall subjects within any the dominions of vs, our heires or successours, to all intents, constructions and purposes, whatsoever, as if they, and every of them, were borne within the realme of England. And ffurther, know ye, that wee, of our more abundant grace, certain knowledge and meere motion, have given, graunted and confirmed, and, by these presents, for vs, our heires and successours, doe give, graunt and confirme, vnto the sayd Governour and Company, and theire successours, all that parte of our dominiones in New-England, in America, conteyneing the Nahantick and Nanhyganset Bay, and countryes and partes adjacent, bounded on the west, or westerly, to the middle or channel of a river there, commonly called and known by the name of Pawcatuck, alias Pawcawtuck river, and soe along the sayd river, as the greater or middle streame thereof reacheth or lyes vpp into the north countrye, northward, unto the head thereoof, and from thence, by a streight lyne drawn due north, vntill itt meets with the south lyne of the Massachusetts Collonie; and on the north, or northerly, by the aforesayd south or southerly lyne of the Massachusettes Collony or Plantation, and extending towards the east, or eastwardly, three English miles to the east and north-east of the most eastern and north-eastern parts of the aforesayd Narragansett Bay, as the sayd bay lyeth or extendeth itself from the ocean on the south, or southwardly, vnto the mouth of the river which runneth towards the towne of Providence, and from thence along the eastwardly side or banke of the sayd river (higher called by the name of Seacunck river), vp to the ffalls called Patuckett ffalls, being the most westwardly lyne of Plymouth Collony, and soe from the sayd ffalls, in a streight lyne, due north, untill itt meete with the aforesayd line of the Massachusetts Collony; and bounded on the south by the ocean: and, in particular, the lands belonging to the townes of Providence, Pawtuxet, Warwicke, Misquammacok, alias Pawcatuck, and the rest vpon the maine land in the tract aforesayd, together with Rhode-Island, Blocke-Island, and all the rest of the islands and banks in the Narragansett Bay, and bordering vpon the coast of the tract aforesayd (Ffisher's Island only excepted), together with all firme lands, soyles, grounds, havens. ports, rivers, waters, ffishings, mines royall, and all other mynes, mineralls, precious stones, quarries, woods, wood-grounds, rocks, slates, and all and singular other commodities, jurisdictions, royalties, priviledges, franchises, preheminences and hereditaments, whatsoever, within the sayd tract, bounds, landes, and islands, aforesayd, or to them or any of them belonging, or in any wise appertaining: *to have and to hold the same*, vnto the sayd Governour and Company, and their successours, forever, vpon trust, for the vse and benefitt of themselves and their associates, ffreemen of the sayd Collony, their heires and assignes, to be holden of vs, our heires and successours, as of the Mannor of East-Greenwich, in our county of Kent, in free and common soccage, and not in capite, nor by knight service; yeilding and paying therefor, to vs, our heires and successours, only the ffifth part of all the oare of gold and silver which, from tyme to tyme, and att all tymes hereafter, shall bee there gotten, had or obtained, in lieu and satisfaction of all services, duties, ffynes, forfeitures, made or to be made, claimes and demands, whatsoever, to bee to vs, our heires or successours, therefor or thereout rendered, made or paid; any graunt, or clause in a late graunt, to the Governour and Company of Connecticutt Colony, in America, to the contrary thereof in any wise notwithstanding; the aforesayd Pawcatuck river haveing byn yielded, after much debate, for the fixed and certain boundes betweene these our sayd Colonies, by the agents thereof; whoe have alsoe agreed, that the sayd Pawcatuck river shall bee alsoe called alias Norrogansett or Narrogansett river; and, to prevent future disputes, that otherwise might arise thereby, forever hereafter shall bee construed, deemed and taken to bee the Narragansett river in our late graunt to Connecticutt Colony mentioned as the easterly bounds of that Colony. *And further*, our will and pleasure is, that in all matters of publique controversy which may fall out betweene our Colony of Providence Plantations, and the rest of our Colonies in New-England, itt shall and may bee lawfull to and for the Governour and Company of the sayd Colony of Providence Plantations to make their appeales therein to vs, our heirs and successours, for redresse in such cases, within this our realme of England: and that itt shall bee lawfull to and for the inhabitants of the sayd Colony of Providence Plantations, without let or molestation, to passe and repasse with freedome, into and thorough the rest of the English Collonies, vpon their lawfull and civill occasions, and to converse, and hold commerce and trade, with such of the inhabitants of our other English Collonies as shall bee willing to admitt them thereunto, they behaveing themselves peaceably among them; any act, clause or sentence, in any of the sayd Collonies provided, or that shall bee provided, to the contrary in anywise notwithstanding. *And lastly*, wee doe, for vs, our heires and successours, ordeyne and graunt vnto the sayd Governor and Company, and their successours, and by these presents, that these our letters patent shall be firme, good, effectuall and available in all things in the lawe, to all intents, constructions and purposes whatsoever, according to our true intent and meaning hereinbefore declared; and shall bee construed, reputed and adjudged in all cases most favorably on the behalfe, and for the benefitt and behoofe, of the sayd Governor and Company, and their successours; although *express mention* of the true yearly value or certainty of the premises, or any of them, or of any other gifts or graunts by vs, or by any of our progenitors or predecessors, heretofore made to the sayd Governor and Company of the English Colony of Rhode-Island and Providence Flantations, in the Narragansett Bay, New-England, in America, in these presents is not made, or any statute, act, ordinance, provision, proclamation or restriction, heretofore had, made, enacted, ordeyned or provided, or any other matter, cause or thing whatsoever, to the contrary thereof in anywise notwithstanding. *In witnes* whereof, wee have caused these our letters to bee made patent. *Witnes* our Selfe att Westminster, the eighth day of July, in the ffifteenth yeare of our reigne.

By the King:

HOWARD.

SELECTED DOCUMENTS

The documents selected for this section have been chosen to reflect the interests or attitudes of the contemporary observer or writer. Documents relating specifically to the constitutional development of Rhode Island will be found in volume eight of <u>Sources and Documents of United States Constitutions</u>, a companion reference collection to the Columbia University volumes previously cited.

ROGER WILLIAMS IN RHODE ISLAND - 1634

Source: <u>America. Great Crises In Our History Told By Its Makers</u>. Chicago: Issued By Americanization Department, Veterans of Foreign Wars, 1925.

ROGER WILLIAMS IN RHODE ISLAND

By Nathaniel Morton

IN 1669 the commissioners of the New England colonies requested Nathaniel Morton, Secretary of the Massachusetts Bay Colony, to compile a history of New England. He called the work which he published at Cambridge, Massachusetts, "New England's Memorial, or a Brief Relation of the Most Remarkable and Memorable Passages of the Providence of God Manifested to the Planters of New England."

This narrative, from which we have taken our account of Roger Williams, was often reprinted both in England and the colonies, and was the chief source of information about the period until recent discoveries of other documents, letters, diaries, etc. Morton lived in the home of Governor Bradford and was strongly prejudiced against Roger Williams for seceding from the Puritan manner of life and mode of religious thought, and that Morton could find nothing worse to say about him, is an eloquent testimonial to the character of Williams.

IN the year 1634 Mr. Roger Williams removed from Plymouth to Salem: he had lived about three years at Plymouth, where he was well accepted as an assistant in the ministry to Mr. Ralph Smith, then pastor of the church there, but by degrees venting of divers of his own singular opinions, and seeking to impose them upon others, he not finding such a concurrence as he expected, he desired his dismission to the Church of Salem, which though some were unwilling to, yet through the prudent counsel of Mr. Brewster (the ruling elder there) fearing that his continuance amongst them might cause division, and [thinking that] there being then many able men in the Bay, they would better deal with him then

[than] themselves could . . . the Church of Plymouth consented to his dismission, and such as did adhere to him were also dismissed, and removed with him, or not long after him, to Salem. . . .

But he having in one year's time filled that place with principles of rigid separation, and tending to Anabaptistry, the prudent magistrates of the Massachusetts jurisdiction, sent to the church of Salem, desiring them to forbear calling him to office, which they not hearkening to, was a cause of much disturbance; for Mr. Williams had begun, and then being in office, he proceeded more vigorously to vent many dangerous opinions, as among many others these were some; That it is not lawful for an unregenerate man to pray, nor to take an oath, and in special, not the oath of fidelity to the Civil Government; nor was it lawful for a godly man to have communion either in family prayer, or in an oath with such as they judged unregenerate: and therefore he himself refused the oath of fidelity, and taught others so to do; also, that it was not lawful so much as to hear the godly ministers of England, when any occasionally went thither; and therefore he admonished any church-members that had done so, as for heinous sin: also he spoke dangerous words against the Patent, which was the foundation of the Government of the Massachusetts Colony: also he affirmed, that the magistrates had nothing to do in matters of the first table [of the commandments], but only the second; and that there should be a general and unlimited toleration of all religions, and for any man to be punished for any matters of his conscience, was persecution. . . .

He persisted, and grew more violent in his way, insomuch as he staying at home in his own house, sent a letter, which was delivered and read in the public church assembly, the scope of which was to give them notice, That if the church of Salem would not separate not only from the churches of Old England, but the churches of New England too, he would separate from them: the more prudent and sober part of the church being amazed at his way, could not yield unto him: whereupon he never came to the church assembly more, professing separation from them as antichristian, and not only so, but he withdrew all private religious communion from any that would hold communion with the church there, insomuch as he would not pray nor give thanks at meals with his own wife nor any of his family, because they went to the church assemblies . . . which the prudent magistrates understanding, and seeing things grow more and more towards a general division and disturbance, after all other means used in vain, they passed a sentence of banishment against him out of the Massachusetts Colony, as against a disturber of the peace, both of the church and commonwealth.

After which Mr. Williams sat down in a place called Providence, out of the Massachusetts jurisdiction, and was followed by many of the members of the church of Salem, who did zealously adhere to him, and who cried out of the persecution that was against him: some others also resorted to him from other parts. They had not been long there together, but from rigid separation they fell to Anabaptistry, renouncing the baptism which they had received in their infancy, and taking up another baptism, and so began a church in that way; but Mr. Williams stopped not there long, for after some time he told the people that had followed him, and joined with him in a new baptism, that he was out of the way himself, and had misled them, for he did not find that there was any upon earth that could administer baptism, and therefore their last baptism was a nullity, as well as their first; and therefore they must lay down all, and wait for the coming of new apostles: and so they dissolved themselves, and turned seekers, keeping that one principle, that every one should have liberty to worship God according to the light of their own consciences; but otherwise not owning any churches or ordinances of God anywhere upon earth.

RHODE ISLAND AND PIRACY - 1699

This letter from Governor Samuel Cranston to the Lords of Trade indicates how the government has dealt with pirates.

Source: Albert Bushnell Hart, ed. *American History Told By Contemporaries*. New York: The Macmillan Company, 1921. Vol. I, 49-51.

RIGHT Honorable: Your letter bearing date Whitehall, October the 25th, 1698, came to our hands the 5th of April last, as likewise the duplicate of the same, we received the same day; wherein your Lordships do signify your observation of the long interval between the date of your letter, the 9th of February, 1698-9, and our-answer to the same.

May it please your Lordships: We shall not justify ourselves wherein we have been remiss, or negligent in that affair; and hope your Lordships will not impute any thing of contempt in us for the same; and we shall for the future endeavor to be more dilligent and observant in returning your Lordships an answer, and giving an account of the affairs of this government. But we having no shipping that sails directly from this Collony, and many times we are disappointed for want of timely notice from other places, the which has been a great disappointment to us in the performance of our duty to your Lordships.

Your Lordships are also pleased to signify that our letter was principally in vindication of our conduct in relation to piracies and pirates, &c. We hope your Lordships will put that constructions upon our writing, that we do not vindicate ourselves, wherein we have ignorantly erred, or for want of better knowledge and a right method we have gone out of the due form and practice your Lordships have now prescribed for us; and wherein we did or do vindicate ourselves, it is in our innocency, and it's said sins of ignorance ought to be forgiven. · And we do humbly beg your Lordships' pardon for the same, hoping for the future to be more circumspect. Your Lordships having been so favorable as to give us directions and instructions, the which we accept as a most bountifull favor from you, and shall with our best endeavors follow the same accordingly.

Your Lordships are also pleased to require a copy of all private commissions which have been granted to any persons from this government, with the bonds, &c. And in obedience to your Lordships' command, we have herewith sent copies of such commissions (if they may properly be so called), they being only defensive, and were granted by the Deputy Governor (contrary to the mind of the then Governor), and he not knowing the due form and method in such cases, took no bonds, concluding as he hath solemnly declared, that they were bound upon a merchandizing voyage; their design being unknown to the authority.

Your Lordships are further pleased to require copies of the tryall of George Cutler and Robert Munday, with all proceedings from first to last, relating to the same; and of all other persons and things in the like case. Likewise a copy of the laws and Acts of this government, all which we have accordingly done. Humbly submitting ourselves to your Lordships' favorable constructions upon any thing that may therein be found amiss; we being wholly ruled and governed by the good and wholesome [laws] of our Mother, the kingdom of England, as far as the constitution of our place will bear; and we doubt not, but your Lordships are sensible that in these remote parts, we cannot in every puncttillo follow the niceties of the laws of England; but it will be a great damage to his Majesty's interest in the settling and peopling the country.

We do also acknowledge the receipt of your Lordships' letter bearing date Whitehall, February the 3d, 1698-9, with his Majesty's Instructions, relating to the observation of the Acts of trade, &c.; all which we kindly accept, and shall with the best of our endeavors comply with the same, and we do further acknowledge the receipt of a letter bearing date Whitehall, January the 24th, 1698-9 (the which came to our hands the 24th instant), wherein his Majesty gives us to understand, that severall ships of force have been fitted out of Scotland, with an intent to settle in some parts of America, contrary to his Majesty's knowledge, forbidding of us to hold any correspondency with them, whilst they are engaged in the aforesaid enterprise; commanding us to send your Lordships an account of our proceeds therein. In obedience to which, we forthwith issued out a Proclamation concerning the same, a copy of which, we herewith send you, and it shall be our further endeavor to see it duly executed.

And may it please your Lordships to accept this further information: that on the beginning of April last, arrived a ship upon our coast, which was by the men that did belong to her, sunk, as they have since confessed. It was a hagboat, of about four hundred tons, belonging to London, bound for the Island of Borneo, in the East India, whereof one Capt'n Gullop was Commander. And at the Island of Polonoys, near the Island of Sumatra, their Commander being on shore with severall others, the boatswain's mate of said ship, one Bradish, with severall others combined, and run away with her, leaving their Commander and severall others, on shore, at said Island of Polonoys.

And for your Lordships' better information, we have herewith sent you the examination of one of the men, now a prisoner in his Majesty's jail in this government, who after the sinking of the said ship, distributed themselves into severall parts of this country, and are all taken and secured in the severall governments, except one, with the greatest part of their money that they brought with them.

We having in our hands to the value of twelve hundred pounds, or thereabouts; all which we shall secure till further orders from your Lordships, we having used all the dilligence we can for discovering what more may be distributed about the country.

We shall always for time to come be very observant in following your Lordships, advice and Instructions, in all cases relating to his Majesty's interest, and once more humbly begging your Lordships' favorable constructions in what of weakness may appear in us. We being a plain and mean sort of people, yet true and loyall subjects to his Most Excellent Majesty, King William, and we hope time will make manifest the same to your Lordships, we being not insensible of the many enemies we have, who hath and do make it their business to render us (to his Majesty and your Lordships), as ridiculous as they can, and to present things to your Lordships quite contrary to what they are or were. For instance, there is one Esquire Randolph, who was employed by the Commissioners of his Majesty's Customs, who did publickly declare he would be a means to eclipse us of our priviledges; and we know he picked up severall false reports against us. But we do not doubt your Lordships will in time have a further insight and knowledge of such men's actions, and we humbly beg of your Lordships, that you will not entertain any reports against us, so as to give any determination on the same, to our ill conveniency till we can have liberty to answer for ourselves; we having commissionated and appointed Jahleel Brenton, Esq'r (his Majesty's late Collector of his Customs in these parts), our Agent to answer to what shall be objected against us, or in any other matter or thing, relating to this his Majesty's Collony, begging your Lordships' favor towards him in what shall appear just and right.

So having not further to offer to your Lordships at present, but humbly submitting ourselves to his Most Excellent Majesty, and your

Lordships' favorable constructions of what herein shall appear amiss; wishing his Majesty a long and peaceable reign, and your Lordships health and prosperity under his government.

Your Lordships' most humble servants,

SAMUEL CRANSTON, Governor.

Newport, on Rhode Island, the 27th of May, 1699.

John Russell Bartlett, editor, *Records of the Colony of Rhode Island, and Providence Plantations, in New England* (Providence, 1858), III, 373-375

PROCEEDINGS OF THE GENERAL ASSEMBLY OF RHODE ISLAND - 1723

These minutes indicate the various aspects of colonial affairs.

Source: Albert Bushnell Hart, ed. *American History Told By Contemporaries*. New York: The Macmillan Company, 1921. Vol. I, 173-174.

THE Hon. Samuel Cranston, Governor.
Richard Ward, recorder.
Col. William Wanton, speaker.
Mr. John Coddington, clerk.

An Act for the better securing the pirates, now in His Majesty's jail, in Newport.

Forasmuch as there are thirty pirates brought into this harbor, by Capt. Solegarr, commander of His Majesty's ship the Grey Hound, and now in His Majesty's jail, in Newport, and it being suspected that they may endeavor to escape from thence, unless they are watched and guarded by night; —

For the preventing of which, be it enacted by the General Assembly, and by the authority of the same it is enacted, that the field officers of the regiment of the militia on the islands, shall, and they are hereby empowered to order and set a military watch of such and so many men as they shall deem needful and necessary, to secure the said pirates from making their escape if attempted, and to set such penalties on default of not watching, as to them shall seem needful; and that the charge of the watch be paid out of the general treasury; any former law, custom or usage to the contrary hereof, in any wise notwithstanding.

Voted, that £100, be remitted out of the general treasury, to our agent in Great Britain, for the service of the colony; and Col. Wm. Coddington and the general treasurer procure bills of exchange or silver, to that value, and deliver it to the Governor, who is to send it to our agent.

Voted, that the £123, odd money, in the hands of Mr. Robert Gardner, late naval officer, be paid by him to Capt. Simon Ray, to and for the use of New Shoreham, to assist them in rebuilding their pier, they building it in two years' time.

Voted, that the sum of £642 12s. 1d., of torn ragged bills in the treasury, be burnt in the presence of this Assembly; and it was burnt accordingly.

Voted, that the general treasurer get the colony house repaired, and refitted where needful; and the charges to be paid out of the general treasury.

Voted, that Mr. Daniel Updike, the attorney general, be, and he hereby is ordered, appointed and empowered to gather in the money due to this colony, for the importation of negroes, and to prosecute, sue and implead such person or persons as shall refuse to pay the same; and that he be allowed five shillings per head, for every slave that shall be hereafter imported into this colony, out of the impost money; and that he be also allowed ten per cent. more for all such money as he shall recover of the outstanding debts; and in all respects to have the like power as was given to the naval officer by the former act.

This Assembly is adjourned to the second Tuesday of September next ensuing.

God save the King.

John Russell Bartlett, editor, *Records of the Colony of Rhode Island and Providence Plantations, in New England* (Providence, 1859), IV, 329-330.

MEMORIAL FROM RHODE ISLAND - 1789

The following memorial discusses a proposed commercial union with the United States because Rhode Island had failed to ratify the Constitution.

Source: Herman V. Ames, ed. State Documents on Federal Relations: The States and the United States. Philadelphia: Published by The Department of History of the University of Pennsylvania, 1906.

STATE DOCUMENTS

ON

FEDERAL RELATIONS:

THE STATES AND THE UNITED STATES.

In June of 1789, the Rhode Island Assembly for the sixth time defeated a proposition to call a convention to consider the ratification of the Federal Constitution, but hoping to avert hostile tariff legislation by Congress, it had passed in May an impost law providing for the collection of the same duties on imports as Congress might lay upon imports into the Union. In September, after re-enacting the law passed by Congress (July 31, 1 *U. S. Stat. at Large*, 48), they sent the following memorial, an overture for a commercial union. Congress, anticipating the receipt of the memorial, passed an act suspending the impost law in favor of Rhode Island and North Carolina until January 15, 1790. (Sept. 15, 1 *U. S. Stat. at Large*, 100. Memorial received, Sept. 26, *Senate Journal*, 1 *Cong.*, 89 (ed. 1820).) Finally the Rhode Island Assembly called a convention for March 1, 1790, and requested a further suspension of the revenue laws. Congress granted an extension until April 1. The convention, however, adjourned without completing its work to May 24. In consequence of its action, the Senate on May 18 passed a bill prohibiting all commercial intercourse with Rhode Island after the 1st of July next, and authorizing the government to demand of that State the payment of its portion of the continental debt without delay. (*Annals of Cong.*, 1, 976; *S. J.*, 1 *Cong.*, 142.) This attitude of the Senate, together with the open threats of coercion in the public press, apparently had an important influence on the convention. That body ratified the constitution, May 29, 1790, by a vote of 34 to 32, also proposing a series of amendments.

References: The text is from *Rhode Island Colonial Records*, X, 356, also slightly changed in *American State Papers, Miscellaneous*, I, 10. For the history, of prime importance is F. G. Bates, *Rhode Island and the Formation of the Union*, Chaps. V, VI (N. Y., 1898); cf. Arnold's *Rhode Island*, II, 536-564 (4th ed.); Curtis, *Constitution*, II, 598-604 (ed. 1860), or I, 692-697 (ed. 1897); Elliot's *Debates*, I, 336, 337.

To the President, Senate and House of Representatives of the eleven United States of America, in Congress assembled:

The critical situation in which the people of this state are placed, engage us to make these assurances, in the behalf of their attachment and friendship to their sister states, and of their disposition to cultivate mutual harmony and friendly intercourse. They know themselves to be a handful, comparatively viewed, and although they now stand as it were, alone, they have not separated themselves, or departed from the principles of that Confederation which was formed by the sister states, in their struggle for freedom and in the hour of danger. They seek by this *memorial* to call to your remembrance the hazard which we have run, the hardships we have endured, the treasures we have spent, and the *blood* we have lost together in one common cause, and especially the object we had in view—the preservation of our *liberty*—wherein ability considered they may truly say, they were equal in exertions with the foremost. The effects whereof in great embarrassments and other distresses, consequent thereon, we have since experienced with severity, which common sufferings and common danger we hope and trust will yet form a bond of union and friendship not easily to be broken. Our not having acceded to or adopted the new system of government found and adopted by most of our sister states, we doubt not have given uneasiness to them. That we have not seen our way clear to do it, consistent with our idea of the principle upon which we all embarked together, has also given *pain* to us; we have not doubted but we might thereby avoid present difficulties, but we have apprehended future mischief. The people of this state from its first settlement have been accustomed and strongly attached to a democratical form of government. They have read in the constitution an approach toward that form of government from which we have lately dissolved our connection at so much hazard of expense of life and treasure,—they have seen with pleasure the administration thereof, from the most important trusts downward, committed to men who have highly merited, and in whom the people of the United States place *unbounded confidence*. Yet, even on this circumstance, in itself so fortunate, they have apprehended danger by way of precedent. Can it be thought strange then, that with these impressions, they should wait to see the proposed system organized and in operation, to see what further checks and securities would be agreed to, etc. [and] established by way of *amendments* before they would adopt it as a constitution of government for themselves and their posterity?

These amendments we believe have already afforded some relief and satisfaction to the minds of the people of this state: And we earnestly look for the time, when they may with clearness and safety, be again united with their sister states under a constitution and form of government so well poised, as neither to need alteration or be liable thereto by a majority only of nine states out of *thirteen*, a circumstance which may possibly take place against the sense of a majority of the people of the United States. We are sensible of the extremes to which democratical government is sometimes liable; something of which we have lately experienced, but we esteem them temporary and partial evils compared with the loss of liberty and the rights of a free people. Neither do we apprehend they will be marked with severity by our sister states, when it is considered that during the late trouble, the whole United States, notwithstanding their joint wisdom and efforts, fell into the like misfortune. That from our extraordinary exertions, this state was left in a situation nearly as embarrassing at that during the war. That in the measures which were adopted, government unfortunately had not the aid and support from the monied interest, which our sister states of New York and the Carolinas experienced under similar circumstances, and especially when it is considered that upon some abatement of that fermentation in the minds of the people which is so common in the collision of sentiments and of parties, a disposition appears to provide a remedy for the difficulties we have labored under on that account.

We are induced to hope that we shall not be altogether considered as foreigners, having no particular affinity or connection with the United States. But that trade and commerce upon which the prosperity of this state much depends, will be preserved as free and open between this and the *United* States as our different situations at present can possibly admit. Earnestly desiring and proposing to adopt such commercial regulations on our part as shall not tend to defeat the collection of the revenue of the United States, but rather to act in conformity to, or corporate [co-operate] therewith, and desiring also to give the strongest assurances that we shall during our present situation use our utmost endeavors to be in preparation, from time to time, to answer our proportion of such part of the interest or principal of the foreign and domestic debt, as the United States shall judge expedient to pay and discharge.

We feel ourselves attached by the strongest ties of friendship, kindred and of interest with our sister states, and we cannot without the greatest reluctance look to any other quarter for those advantages of commercial intercourse which we conceve to be more natural and recprocal between them and us.[1]

THE PEOPLE'S CONSTITUTION - 1841

The unauthorized convention which met from October 4 to November 18 drew up The People's Constitution which modified the Charter and granted more rights to the people.

Source: Arthur May Mowry. <u>The Dorr War</u>. Providence, R. I.: Preston & Rounds Co., 1901, 322-346.

"THE PEOPLE'S CONSTITUTION."

WE, the people of the State of Rhode Island and Providence Plantations, grateful to Almighty God for his blessing vouchsafed to the "lively experiment" of religious and political freedom here "held forth" by our venerated ancestors, and earnestly imploring the favor of his gracious providence towards this our attempt to secure upon a permanent foundation the advantages of well ordered and rational liberty, and to enlarge and transmit to our successors the inheritance that we have received, do ordain and establish the following constitution of government for this State.

ARTICLE I.

Declaration of Principles and Rights.

1. In the spirit and in the words of Roger Williams, the illustrious founder of this State, and of his venerated associates, we declare "that this government shall be a democracy," or government of the people, "by the major consent" of the same "only in civil things." The will of the people shall be expressed by representatives freely chosen, and returning at fixed periods to their constituents. This State shall be, and forever remain, as in the design of its founder, sacred to "soul liberty," to the rights of conscience, to freedom of thought, of expression, and of action, as hereinafter set forth and secured.

2. All men are created free and equal, and are endowed by their Creator with certain natural, inherent, and inalienable rights; among which are life, liberty, the acquisition of property, and the pursuit of happiness. Government cannot create or bestow these rights, which are the gift of God; but it is instituted for the stronger and surer defence of the same, that men may safely enjoy the rights of life and liberty, securely possess and transmit property, and, so far as laws avail, may be successful in the pursuit of happiness.

3. All political power and sovereignty are originally vested in, and of right belong to, the people. All free governments are founded in their authority, and are established for the greatest good of the whole number. The people have therefore an unalienable and indefeasible right, in their original, sovereign, and unlimited capacity, to ordain and institute government, and in the same capacity to alter, reform, or totally change the same, whenever their safety or happiness requires.

4. No favor or disfavor ought to be shown in legislation toward any man, or party, or society, or religious denomination. The laws should be made not for the good of the few, but of the many; and the burdens of the State ought to be fairly distributed among its citizens.

5. The diffusion of useful knowledge, and the cultivation of a sound morality in the fear of God, being of the first importance in a republican State, and indispensable to the maintenance of its liberty, it shall be an imperative duty of the legislature to promote the establishment of free schools, and to assist in the support of public education.

6. Every person in this State ought to find a certain remedy, by having recourse to the laws, for all injuries or wrongs which may be done to his rights of person, property, or character. He ought to obtain right and justice freely and without purchase, completely and without denial, promptly and without delay, conformably to the laws.

7. The right of the people to be secure in their persons, houses, papers, and possessions, against unreasonable searches and seizures, shall not be violated; and no warrant shall issue but on complaint in writing upon probable cause, supported by oath or affirmation, and describing as nearly as may be the place to be searched, and the person or things to be seized.

8. No person shall be held to answer to a capital or other infamous charge, unless on indictment by a grand jury, except in cases arising in the land or naval forces, or in the militia, when in actual service, in time of war or public danger. No person shall be tried, after an acquittal, for the same crime or offence.

9. Every man being presumed to be innocent until pronounced guilty by the law, all acts of severity, that are not necessary to secure an accused person, ought to be repressed.

10. Excessive bail shall not be required, nor excessive fines imposed, nor cruel or unusual punishments inflicted; and all punishments ought to be proportioned to the offence.

11. All prisoners shall be bailable upon sufficient surety, unless for capital offences, when the proof is evident or the presumption great. The privilege of the writ of habeas corpus shall not be suspended, unless when, in cases of rebellion or invasion, the public safety shall require it.

12. In all criminal prosecutions, the accused shall have the privilege of a speedy and public trial, by an impartial jury; be informed of the nature and cause of the accusation; be confronted with the witnesses against him; have compulsory process to obtain them in his favor, and at the public expense, when necessary; have the assistance of counsel in his defence, and be at liberty to speak for himself. Nor shall he be deprived of his life, liberty, or property, unless by the judgment of his peers, or the law of the land.

13. The right of trial by jury shall remain inviolate, and in all criminal cases the jury shall judge both of the law and of the facts.

14. Any person in this State, who may be claimed to be held to labor or service, under the laws of any other State, Territory, or District, shall be entitled to a jury trial, to ascertain the validity of such claim.

15. No man in a court of common law shall be required to criminate himself.

16. Retrospective laws, civil and criminal, are unjust and oppressive, and shall not be made.

17. The people have a right to assemble in a peaceable manner without molestation or restraint, to consult upon the public welfare; a right to give

instructions to their Senators and Representatives; and a right to apply to those invested with the powers of government for the redress of grievances, for the repeal of injurious laws, for the correction of faults of administration, and for all other purposes.

18. The liberty of the press being essential to the security of freedom in a State, any citizen may publish his sentiments on any subject, being responsible for the abuse of that liberty; and in all trials for libel, both civil and criminal, the truth, spoken from good motives, and for justifiable ends, shall be a sufficient defence to the person charged.

19. Private property shall not be taken for public uses without just compensation, nor unless the public good require it; nor under any circumstances, until compensation shall have been made, if required.

20. The military shall always be held in strict subordination to the civil authority.

21. No soldier shall, in time of peace, be quartered in any house, without the consent of the owner; nor in time of war, but in manner to be prescribed by law.

22. Whereas Almighty God hath created the mind free, and all attempts to influence it by temporal punishments, or burdens, or by civil incapacitations, tend to beget habits of hypocrisy and meanness: and whereas a principal object of our venerated ancestors in their migration to this country, and their settlement of this State, was, as they expressed it, to hold forth a lively experiment, that a flourishing civil State may stand, and be best maintained, with full liberty in religious concernments: We therefore DECLARE that no man shall be compelled to frequent or support any religious worship, place, or ministry whatsoever, nor be enforced, restrained, molested, or burdened in his body or goods, nor disqualified from holding any office, nor otherwise suffer, on account of his religious belief; and that all men shall be free to profess, and by argument to maintain, their opinions in matters of religion; and that the same shall in nowise diminish, enlarge, or affect their civil capacities; and that all other religious rights and privileges of the people of this State, as now enjoyed, shall remain inviolate and inviolable.

23. No witness shall be called in question before the legislature, nor any court of this State, nor before any magistrate or other person authorized to

administer an oath or affirmation, for his or her religious belief, or opinions, or any part thereof; and no objection to a witness, on the ground of his or her religious opinions, shall be entertained or received.

24. The citizens shall continue to enjoy and freely exercise all the rights of fishery, and privileges of the shore, to which they have been heretofore entitled under the charter and usages of this State.

25. The enumeration of the foregoing rights shall not be construed to impair nor deny others retained by the people.

ARTICLE II.
Of Electors and the Right of Suffrage.

1. Every white male citizen of the United States, of the age of twenty-one years, who has resided in this State for one year, and in any town, city, or district of the same for six months, next preceding the election at which he offers to vote, shall be an elector of all officers who are elected, or may hereafter be made eligible by the people. But persons in the military, naval or marine service of the United States, shall not be considered as having such established residence, by being stationed in any garrison, barrack, or military place in any town or city in this State.

2. Paupers and persons under guardianship, insane, or lunatic, are excluded from the electoral right; and the same shall be forfeited on conviction of bribery, forgery, perjury, theft, or other infamous crime, and shall not be restored unless by an act of the General Assembly.

3. No person who is excluded from voting, for want of the qualification first named in section first of this article, shall be taxed, or be liable to do military duty; provided that nothing in said first article shall be so construed as to exempt from taxation any property or persons now liable to be taxed.

4. No elector who is not possessed of, and assessed for, ratable property in his own right, to the amount of one hundred and fifty dollars, or who shall have neglected or refused to pay any tax assessed upon him, in any town, city, or district, for one year preceding the town, city, ward, or district meeting at which he shall offer to vote, shall be entitled to vote on any question of taxation, or the expenditure of public moneys in such town, city or district, until the same be paid.

5. In the city of Providence, and other cities, no person shall be eligible to the office of mayor, alderman, or common councilman, who is not taxed, or who shall have neglected or refused to pay his tax, as provided in the preceding section.

6. The voting for all officers chosen by the people, except town or city officers, shall be by ballot; that is to say, by depositing a written or printed ticket in the ballot-box, without the name of the voter written thereon. Town or city officers shall be chosen by ballot, on the demand of any two persons entitled to vote for the same.

7. There shall be a strict registration of all qualified voters in the towns and cities of the State; and no person shall be permitted to vote, whose name has not been entered upon the list of voters before the polls are opened.

8. The General Assembly shall pass all necessary laws for the prevention of fraudulent voting by persons not having an actual, permanent residence, or home, in the State, or otherwise disqualified according to this constitution; for the careful registration of all voters, previously to the time of voting; for the prevention of frauds upon the ballot-box; for the preservation of the purity of elections; and for the safe-keeping and accurate counting of votes; to the end that the will of the people may be freely and fully expressed, truly ascertained, and effectually exerted, without intimidation, suppression, or unnecessary delay.

9. The electors shall be exempted from arrest on days of election, and one day before, and one day after the same, except in cases of treason, felony, or breach of the peace.

10. No person shall be eligible to any office by the votes of the people, who does not possess the qualifications of an elector.

ARTICLE III.

Of the Distribution of Powers.

1. The powers of the government shall be distributed into three departments—the legislative, the executive, and the judicial.

2. No person or persons connected with one of these departments shall exercise any of the powers belonging to either of the others, except in cases herein directed or permitted.

ARTICLE IV.

Of the Legislative Department.

1. The legislative power shall be vested in two distinct Houses: the one to be called the House of Representatives, the other the Senate, and both together the General Assembly. The concurrent votes of the two Houses shall be necessary to the enactment of laws; and the style of their laws shall be: Be it enacted by the General Assembly as follows.

2. No member of the General Assembly shall be eligible to any civil office under the authority of the State, during the term for which he shall have been elected.

3. If any Representative, or Senator, in the General Assembly of this State, shall be appointed to any office under the government of the United States, and shall accept the same, after his election as such Senator or Representative, his seat shall thereby become vacant.

4. Any person who holds an office under the government of the United States may be elected a member of the General Assembly, and may hold his seat therein, if, at the time of his taking his seat, he shall have resigned said office, and shall declare the same on oath, or affirmation, if required.

5. No member of the General Assembly shall take any fees, be of counsel or act as advocate in any case pending before either branch of the General Assembly, under penalty of forfeiting his seat, upon due proof thereof.

6. Each House shall judge of the election and qualifications of its members; and a majority of all the members of each House, whom the towns and the Senatorial districts are entitled to elect, shall constitute a quorum to do business; but a smaller number may adjourn from day to day, and may compel the attendance of absent members, in such manner, and under such penalties, as each House may have previously prescribed.

7. Each House may determine the rules of its proceedings, punish its members for disorderly behavior, and, with the concurrence of two-thirds of the members elected, expel a member; but not a second time for the same cause.

8. Each House shall keep a journal of its proceedings, and publish the same when required by one-fifth of its members. The yeas and nays of the

members of either House shall, at the desire of any five members present, be entered on the journal.

9. Neither House shall, without the consent of the other, adjourn for more than two days, nor to any other place than that at which the General Assembly is holding its session.

10. The Senators and Representatives shall, in all cases of civil process, be privileged from arrest during the session of the General Assembly, and for two days before the commencement, and two days after the termination of any session thereof. For any speech in debate in either House, no member shall be called in question in any other place.

11. The civil and military officers, heretofore elected in grand committee, shall hereafter be elected annually by the General Assembly, in joint committee, composed of the two Houses of the General Assembly, excepting as is otherwise provided in this constitution; and excepting the captains and subalterns of the militia, who shall be elected by the ballots of the members composing their respective companies, in such manner as the General Assembly may prescribe; and such officers, so elected, shall be approved of and commissioned by the Governor, who shall determine their rank; and, if said companies shall neglect or refuse to make such elections, after being duly notified, then the Governor shall appoint suitable persons to fill such offices.

12. Every bill and every resolution requiring the concurrence of the two Houses (votes of adjournment excepted), which shall have passed both Houses of the General Assembly, shall be presented to the Governor for his revision. If he approve of it, he shall sign and transmit the same to the Secretary of State; but, if not, he shall return it to the House in which it shall have originated, with his objections thereto, which shall be entered at large on their journal. The House shall then proceed to reconsider the bill; and if, after such reconsideration, that House shall pass it by a majority of all the members elected, it shall be sent with the objections to the other House, which shall also reconsider it; and, if approved by that House, by a majority of all the members elected, it shall become a law. If the bill shall not be returned by the Governor within forty-eight hours (Sundays excepted), after it shall have been presented to him, the same shall become a law, in like

manner as if he had signed it, unless the General Assembly by their adjournment, prevent its return; in which case, it shall not be a law.

13. There shall be two sessions of the General Assembly in every year; one session to be held at Newport, on the first Tuesday of June, for the organization of the government, the election of officers, and for other business; and one other session on the first Tuesday of January, to be held at Providence, in the first year after the adoption of this constitution, and in every second year thereafter. In the intermediate years, the January session shall be forever hereafter held in the counties of Washington, Kent, or Bristol, as the General Assembly may determine before their adjournment in June.

ARTICLE V.
Of the House of Representatives.

1. The House of Representatives shall consist of members chosen by the electors in the several towns and cities, in their respective town and ward meetings, annually.

2. The towns and cities shall severally be entitled to elect members according to the apportionment which follows, viz.: Newport to elect five; Warwick, four; Smithfield, five; Cumberland, North Providence, and Scituate, three; Portsmouth, Westerly, New Shoreham, North Kingstown, South Kingstown, East Greenwich, Glocester, West Greenwich, Coventry, Exeter, Bristol, Tiverton, Little Compton, Warren, Richmond, Cranston, Charlestown, Hopkinton, Johnston, Foster, and Burrillville to elect two; and Jamestown, Middletown, and Barrington to elect one.

3. In the city of Providence there shall be six representative districts, which shall be the six wards of said city; and the electors resident in said districts, for the term of three months next preceding the election at which they offer to vote, shall be entitled to elect two Representatives for each district.

4. The General Assembly, in case of great inequality in the population of the wards of the city of Providence, may cause the boundaries of the six representative districts therein to be so altered as to include in each district, as nearly as may be, an equal number of inhabitants.

5. The House of Representatives shall have authority to elect their own Speaker, clerks, and other officers. The oath of office shall be administered to the Speaker by the Secretary of State, or, in his absence, by the Attorney-General.

6. Whenever the seat of a member of the House of Representatives shall be vacated by death, resignation, or otherwise, the vacancy may be filled by a new election.

ARTICLE VI.
Of the Senate.

1. The State shall be divided into twelve senatorial districts; and each district shall be entitled to one Senator, who shall be annually chosen by the electors in his district.

2. The first, second, and third representative districts in the city of Providence shall constitute the first senatorial district; the fourth, fifth, and sixth representative districts in said city, the second district; the town of Smithfield, the third district; the towns of North Providence and Cumberland, the fourth district; the towns of Scituate, Glocester, Burrillville, and Johnston, the fifth district; the towns of Warwick and Cranston, the sixth district; the towns of East Greenwich, West Greenwich, Coventry, and Foster, the seventh district; the towns of Newport, Jamestown, and New Shoreham, the eighth district; the towns of Portsmouth, Middletown, Tiverton, and Little Compton, the ninth district; the towns of North Kingstown and South Kingstown, the tenth district; the towns of Westerly, Charlestown, Exeter, Richmond, and Hopkinton, the eleventh district; the towns of Bristol, Warren, and Barrington, the twelfth district.

3. The Lieutenant-Governor shall be, by virtue of his office, President of the Senate; and shall have a right, in case of an equal division, to vote in the same; and also to vote in joint committee of the two Houses.

4. When the government shall be administered by the Lieutenant-Governor, or he shall be unable to attend as President of the Senate, the Senate shall elect one of their own members President of the same.

5. Vacancies in the Senate, occasioned by death, resignation, or otherwise, may be filled by a new election.

6. The Secretary of State shall be, by virtue of his office, Secretary of the Senate.

ARTICLE VII.

Of Impeachments.

1. The House of Representatives shall have the sole power of impeachment.
2. All impeachments shall be tried by the Senate; and when sitting for that purpose, they shall be on oath or affirmation. No person shall be convicted, except by a vote of two-thirds of the members elected. When the Governor is impeached, the chief justice of the supreme court shall preside, with a casting vote in all preliminary questions.
3. The Governor, and all other executive and judicial officers, shall be liable to impeachment; but judgments, in such cases, shall not extend further than to removal from office. The party convicted shall, nevertheless, be liable to indictment, trial, and punishment according to law.

ARTICLE VIII.

Of the Executive Department.

1. The chief executive power of this State shall be vested in a Governor, who shall be chosen by the electors, and shall hold his office for one year, and until his successor be duly qualified.
2. No person holding any office or place under the United States, this State, any other of the United States, or any foreign power, shall exercise the office of Governor.
3. He shall take care that the laws are faithfully executed.
4. He shall be commander-in-chief of the military and naval forces of the State, except when called into the actual service of the United States; but he shall not march nor convey any of the citizens out of the State, without their consent, or that of the General Assembly, unless it shall become necessary in order to march or transport them from one part of the State to another, for the defence thereof.

5. He shall appoint all civil and military officers whose appointment is not by this constitution, or shall not by law, be otherwise provided for.

6. He shall, from time to time, inform the General Assembly of the condition of the State, and recommend to their consideration such measures as he may deem expedient.

7. He may require from any military officer, or any officer in the executive department, information upon any subject relating to the duties of his office.

8. He shall have power to remit forfeitures and penalties, and to grant reprieves, commutation of punishments, and pardons after conviction, except in cases of impeachment.

9. The Governor shall, at stated times, receive for his services a compensation which shall not be increased nor diminished during his continuance in office.

10. There shall be elected, in the same manner as is provided for the election of Governor, a Lieutenant-Governor, who shall continue in office for the same term of time. Whenever the office of Governor shall become vacant by death, resignation, removal from office, or otherwise, the Lieutenant-Governor shall exercise the office of Governor until another Governor shall be duly qualified.

11. Whenever the offices of Governor and Lieutenant-Governor shall both become vacant, by death, resignation, removal from office, or otherwise, the President of the Senate shall exercise the office of Governor until a Governor be duly qualified; and should such vacancies occur during a recess of the General Assembly, and there be no President of the Senate, the Secretary of State shall, by proclamation, convene the Senate, that a President may be chosen to exercise the office of Governor.

12. Whenever the Lieutenant-Governor or President of the Senate shall exercise the office of Governor, he shall receive the compensation of Governor only; and his duties as President of the Senate shall cease while he shall continue to act as Governor; and the Senate shall fill the vacancy by an election from their own body.

13. In case of a disagreement between the two Houses of the General Assembly respecting the time or place of adjournment, the person exercis-

ing the office of Governor may adjourn them to such time or place as he shall think proper; provided that the time of adjournment shall not be extended beyond the first day of the next stated session.

14. The person exercising the office of Governor may, in cases of special necessity, convene the General Assembly at any town or city in this State, at any other time than hereinbefore provided. And, in case of danger from the prevalence of epidemic or contagious diseases, or from other circumstances, in the place in which the General Assembly are next to meet, he may, by proclamation, convene the Assembly at any other place within the State.

15. A Secretary of State, a General Treasurer, and an Attorney-General, shall also be chosen annually, in the same manner, and for the same time, as is herein provided respecting the Governor. The duties of these officers shall be the same as now, or may be hereafter be, prescribed by law. Should there be a failure to choose either of them, or should a vacancy occur in either of their offices, the General Assembly shall fill the place by an election in joint committee.

16. The electors in each county shall, at the annual elections, vote for an inhabitant of the county to be sheriff of said county, for one year, and until a successor be duly qualified. In case no person shall have a majority of the electoral votes of his county for sheriff, the General Assembly, in joint committee, shall elect a sheriff from the two candidates who shall have the greatest number of votes in such county.

17. All commissions shall be in the name of the State of Rhode Island and Providence Plantations, sealed with the seal of the State, and attested by the Secretary.

ARTICLE IX.

General Provisions.

1. This constitution shall be the supreme law of the State; and all laws contrary to, or inconsistent with the same, which may be passed by the General Assembly, shall be null and void.

2. The General Assembly shall pass all necessary laws for carrying this constitution into effect.

3. The judges of all the courts, and all other officers, both civil and military, shall be bound by oath or affirmation to the due observance of this constitution, and of the constitution of the United States.

4. No jurisdiction shall, hereafter, be entertained by the General Assembly in cases of insolvency, divorce, sale of real estate of minors, or appeal from judicial decisions, nor in any other matters appertaining to the jurisdiction of judges and courts of law. But the General Assembly shall confer upon the courts of the State all necessary powers for affording relief in the cases herein named; and the General Assembly shall exercise all other jurisdiction and authority which they have heretofore entertained, and which is not prohibited by, nor repugnant to, this constitution.

5. The General Assembly shall, from time to time, cause estimates to be made of the ratable property of the State, in order to the equitable apportionment of State taxes.

6. Whenever a direct tax is laid by the State, one-sixth part thereof shall be assessed on the polls of the qualified electors: provided that the tax upon a poll shall never exceed the sum of fifty cents; and that all persons who actually perform military duty, or duty in the fire department, shall be exempted from said poll tax.

7. The General Assembly shall have no power hereafter to incur State debts to an amount exceeding the sum of fifty thousand dollars, except in time of war, or in case of invasion, without the express consent of the people. Every proposition for such increase shall be submitted to the electors at the next annual election, or on some day to be set apart for that purpose; and shall not be farther entertained by the General Assembly, unless it receive the votes of a majority of all the persons voting. This section shall not be construed to refer to any money that now is, or hereafter may be, deposited with this State by the General Government.

8. The assent of two-thirds of the members elected to each House of the General Assembly shall be requisite to every bill appropriating the public moneys, or property, for local or private purposes; or for creating, continuing, altering, or renewing any body politic or corporate, banking corporations excepted.

9. Hereafter, when any bill creating, continuing, altering, or renewing any banking corporation, authorized to issue its promissory notes for circula-

tion, shall pass the two Houses of the General Assembly, instead of being sent to the Governor, it shall be referred to the electors for their consideration, at the next annual election, or on some day to be set apart for that purpose, with printed tickets containing the question—Shall said bill (with a brief description of it) be approved or not? and if a majority of the electors voting shall vote to approve said bill, it shall become a law; otherwise not.

10. All grants of incorporation shall be subject to future acts of the General Assembly, in amendment or repeal thereof, or in anywise affecting the same; and this provision shall be inserted in all acts of incorporation hereafter granted.

11. The General Assembly shall exercise, as heretofore, a visitatorial power over corporations. Three bank commissioners shall be chosen at the June session for one year, to carry out the powers of the General Assembly in this respect. And commissioners for the visitation of other corporations, as the General Assembly may deem expedient, shall be chosen at the June session, for the same term of office.

12. No city council, or other government, in any city, shall have power to vote any tax upon the inhabitants thereof, excepting the amount necessary to meet the ordinary public expenses of the same, without first submitting the question of an additional tax, or taxes, to the electors of said city; and a majority of all who vote shall determine the question. But no elector shall be entitled to vote, in any city, upon any question of taxation thus submitted, unless he shall be qualified by the possession, in his own right, of ratable property to the amount of one hundred and fifty dollars, and shall have been assessed thereon to pay a city tax, and shall have paid the same, as provided in section fourth of article two. Nothing in that article shall be so construed as to prevent any elector from voting for town officers, and, in the city of Providence, and other cities, for mayor, aldermen, and members of the common council.

13. The General Assembly shall not pass any law, nor cause any act or thing to be done, in any way to disturb any of the owners or occupants of land in any territory now under the jurisdiction of any other State or States, the jurisdiction whereof may be ceded to or decreed to belong to,

this State; and the inhabitants of such territory shall continue in the full, quiet, and undisturbed enjoyment of their titles to the same, without interference in any way on the part of this State.

ARTICLE X.

Of Elections.

1. The election of the Governor, Lieutenant-Governor, Secretary of State, General Treasurer, Attorney-General, and also of Senators and Representatives to the General Assembly, and of sheriffs of the counties, shall be held on the third Wednesday of April annually.

2. The names of the persons voted for as Governor, Lieutenant-Governor, Secretary of State, General Treasurer, Attorney-General, and sheriffs of the respective counties, shall be put upon one ticket; and the tickets shall be deposited by the electors in a box by themselves. The names of the persons voted for as Senators and as Representatives shall be put upon separate tickets, and the tickets shall be deposited in separate boxes. The polls for all the officers named in this section shall be opened at the same time.

3. All the votes given for Governor, Lieutenant-Governor, Secretary of State, General Treasurer, Attorney-General, sheriffs, and also for Senators, shall remain in the ballot-boxes till the polls be closed. These votes shall then, in open town and ward meetings, and in the presence of at least ten qualified voters, be taken out and sealed up, in separate envelopes, by the moderators and town clerks, and by the wardens and ward clerks, who shall certify the same, and forthwith deliver or send them to the Secretary of State, whose duty it shall be securely to keep the same, and to deliver the votes for State officers and sheriffs to the Speaker of the House of Representatives, after the House shall be organized, at the June session of the General Assembly. The votes last named shall, without delay, be opened, counted, and declared, in such manner as the House of Representatives shall direct; and the oath of office shall be administered to the persons who shall be declared to be elected, by the Speaker of the House of Representatives, and in the presence of the House; provided that the sheriffs may take their engagement before a Senator, judge, or justice of the peace. The votes for

Senators shall be counted by the Governor and Secretary of State within seven days from the day of election; and the Governor shall give certificates to the Senators who are elected.

4. The boxes containing the votes for Representatives to the General Assembly in the several towns shall not be opened till the polls for Representatives are declared to be closed. The votes shall then be declared by the moderator and clerk, who shall announce the result, and give certificates to the persons selected. If there be no election, or not an election of the whole number of Representatives to which the town is entitled, the polls for Representatives may be re-opened, and the like proceedings shall be had, until an election shall take place: provided, however, that an adjournment of the election may be made to a time not exceeding seven days from the first meeting.

5. In the city of Providence, and other cities, the polls for Representatives shall be kept open during the whole time of voting for the day; and the votes in the several wards shall be sealed up, at the close of the meeting, by the wardens and ward clerks, in the presence of at least ten qualified electors, and delivered to the city clerks. The mayor and aldermen of said city or cities, shall proceed to count said votes within two days from the day of election; and if no election, or an election of only a portion of the Representatives whom the representative districts are entitled to elect, shall have taken place, the mayor and aldermen shall order a new election to be held, not more than ten days from the day of the first election; and so on, till the election of Representatives shall be completed. Certificates of election shall be furnished to the persons chosen, by the city clerks.

6. If there be no choice of a Senator or Senators at the annual election, the Governor shall issue his warrant to the town and ward clerks of the several towns and cities in the senatorial district or districts that may have failed to elect, requiring them to open town or ward meetings for another election, on a day not more than fifteen days beyond the time of counting the votes for Senators. If, on the second trial, there shall be no choice of a Senator or Senators, the Governor shall certify the result to the Speaker of the House of Representatives; and the House of Representatives, and as many Senators as shall have been chosen, shall forthwith elect, in joint com-

mittee, a Senator or Senators, from the two candidates who may receive the highest number of votes in each district.

7. If there be no choice for Governor at the annual election, the Speaker of the House of Representatives shall issue his warrant to the clerks of the several towns and cities, requiring them to notify town and ward meetings for another election, on a day to be named by him, not more than thirty nor less than twenty days beyond the time of receiving the report of the committee of the House of Representatives who shall count the votes for Governor. If on this second trial there shall be no choice of a Governor, the two Houses of the General Assembly shall, at their next session, in joint committee, elect a Governor from the two candidates having the highest number of votes, to hold his office for the remainder of the political year, and until his successor be duly qualified.

8. If there be no choice of Governor and Lieutenant-Governor at the annual election, the same proceedings for the choice of a Lieutenant-Governor shall be had as directed in the preceding section: provided, that the second trial for the election of Governor and Lieutenant-Governor shall be on the same day; and also provided, that, if the Governor shall be chosen at the annual election, and the Lieutenant-Governor shall not be chosen, then the last-named officer shall be elected in joint committee of the two Houses, from the two candidates having the highest number of votes, without a further appeal to the electors. The Lieutenant-Governor, elected as provided in this section, shall hold his office as is provided in the preceding section respecting the Governor.

9. All town, city, and ward meetings for the choice of Representatives, justices of the peace, sheriffs, Senators, State officers, Representatives to Congress, and electors of President and Vice-President, shall be notified by the town, city, or ward clerks, at least seven days before the same are held.

10. In all elections held by the people under this constitution, a majority of all the electors voting shall be necessary to the choice of the person or persons voted for.

11. The oath, or affirmation, to be taken by all the officers named in this article shall be the following: You, being elected to the place (of Governor, Lieutenant-Governor, Secretary of State, General Treasurer, Attorney-Gen-

eral, or to the places of Senators or Representatives, or to the office of sheriff or justice of the peace), do solemnly swear, or severally solemnly swear, or affirm, that you will be true and faithful to the State of Rhode Island and Providence Plantations, and that you will support the constitution thereof; that you will support the constitution of the United States; and that you will faithfully and impartially discharge the duties of your aforesaid office, to the best of your abilities and understanding: so help you God! or, this affirmation you make and give upon the peril of the penalty of perjury.

ARTICLE XI.

Of the Judiciary.

1. The judicial power of this State shall be vested in one supreme court, and in such other courts, inferior to the supreme court, as the legislature may, from time to time, ordain and establish; and the jurisdiction of the supreme and of all other courts may, from time to time, be regulated by the General Assembly.

2. Chancery power may be conferred on the supreme court; but no other court exercising chancery powers shall be established in this State, except as is now provided by law.

3. The justices of the supreme court shall be elected in joint committee of the two Houses, to hold their offices for one year, and until their places shall be declared vacant by a resolution to that effect, which shall be voted for by a majority of all the members elected to the House in which it may originate, and be concurred in by the same vote of the other House, without revision by the Governor. Such resolution shall not be entertained at any other than the annual session for the election of public officers; and, in default of the passage thereof at the said session, the judge, or judges, shall hold his or their place or places for another year. But a judge of any court shall be removable from office, if, upon impeachment, he shall be found guilty of any official misdemeanor.

4. In case of vacancy by the death, resignation, refusal, or inability to serve, or removal from the State, of a judge of any court, his place may be filled by the joint committee, until the next annual election; when, if elected, he shall hold his office as herein provided.

5. The justices of the supreme court shall receive a compensation, which shall not be diminished during their continuance in office.

6. The judges of the courts inferior to the supreme court shall be annually elected in joint committee of the two Houses, except as herein provided.

7. There shall be annually elected by each town, and by the several wards in the city of Providence, a sufficient number of justices of the peace, or wardens resident therein, with such jurisdiction as the General Assembly may prescribe. And said justices or wardens (except in the towns of New Shoreham and Jamestown) shall be commissioned by the Governor.

8. The General Assembly may provide that justices of the peace, who are not re-elected, may hold their offices for a time not exceeding ten days beyond the day of the annual election of these officers.

9. The courts of probate in this State, except the supreme court, shall remain as at present established by law, until the General Assembly shall otherwise prescribe.

ARTICLE XII.

Of Education.

1. All moneys which now are, or may hereafter be, appropriated, by the authority of the State, to public education, shall be securely invested, and remain a perpetual fund for the maintenance of free schools in this State; and the General Assembly are prohibited from diverting said moneys or fund from this use, and from borrowing, appropriating, or using the same, or any part thereof, for any other purpose, or under any pretence whatsoever. But the income derived from said moneys or fund shall be annually paid over, by the General Treasurer, to the towns and cities of the State, for the support of said schools, in equitable proportions: provided, however, that a portion of said income may, in the discretion of the General Assembly, be added to the principal of said fund.

2. The several towns and cities shall faithfully devote their portions of said annual distribution to the support of free schools; and, in default thereof, shall forfeit their shares of the same to the increase of the fund.

3. All charitable donations for the support of free schools, and other purposes of public education, shall be received by the General Assembly,

and invested and applied agreeably to the terms prescribed by the donors: provided the same be not inconsistent with the constitution, or with sound public policy; in which case the donation shall not be received.

ARTICLE XIII.

Amendments.

The General Assembly may propose amendments to this constitution by the vote of a majority of all the members elected to each House. Such propositions shall be published in the newspapers of the State; and printed copies of such propositions shall be sent by the Secretary of State, with the names of all the members who shall have voted thereon, with the yeas and nays, to all the town and city clerks in the State; and the said propositions shall be, by said clerks, inserted in the notices by them issued for warning the next annual town and ward meetings in April; and the town and ward clerks shall read said propositions to the electors, when thus assembled, with the names of all the Representatives and Senators, who shall have voted thereon, with the yeas and nays, before the election of Representatives and Senators shall be had. If a majority of all the members elected at said annual meetings, present in each House, shall approve any proposition thus made, the same shall be published as before provided, and then sent to the electors in the mode provided in the act of approval; and, if then approved by a majority of the electors who shall vote in town and ward meetings, to be specially convened for that purpose, it shall become a part of the constitution of the State.

ARTICLE XIV.

Of the Adoption of the Constitution.

1. This constitution shall be submitted to the people, for their adoption or rejection, on Monday, the 27th day of December next, and on the two succeeding days; and all persons voting are requested to deposit in the ballot-boxes printed or written tickets in the following form: I am an American citizen, of the age of twenty-one years, and have my permanent residence, or home, in this State. I am (or not) qualified to vote under the existing

laws of this State. I vote for (or against) the constitution formed by the convention of the people, assembled at Providence, and which was proposed to the people by said convention on the 18th day of November, 1841.

2. Every voter is requested to write his name on the face of his ticket; and every person entitled to vote as aforesaid, who, from sickness or other causes, may be unable to attend and vote in the town or ward meetings assembled for voting upon said constitution, on the days aforesaid, is requested to write his name upon a ticket, and to obtain the signature, upon the back of the same, of a person who has given his vote, as a witness thereto. And the moderator, or clerk, of any town or ward meeting convened for the purpose aforesaid, shall receive such vote, on either of the three days next succeeding the three days before named for voting on said constitution.

3. The citizens of the several towns in this State, and of the several wards of the city of Providence, are requested to hold town and ward meetings on the days appointed, and for the purpose aforesaid; and also to choose, in each town and ward, a moderator and clerk, to conduct said meetings, and receive the votes.

4. The moderators and clerks are required to receive, and carefully to keep, the votes of all persons qualified to vote as aforesaid, and to make registers of all the persons voting; which, together with the tickets given in by the voters, shall be sealed up, and returned by said moderators and clerks, with certificates signed and sealed by them, to the clerks of the convention of the people, to be by them safely deposited and kept, and laid before said convention, to be counted and declared at their next adjourned meeting, on the 12th day of January, 1842.

5. This constitution, except so much thereof as relates to the election of the officers named in the sixth section of this article, shall, if adopted, go into operation on the first Tuesday of May, in the year one thousand eight hundred and forty-two.

6. So much of the constitution as relates to the election of the officers named in this section shall go into operation on the Monday before the third Wednesday of April next preceding. The first election under this constitution, of Governor, Lieutenant-Governor, Secretary of State, General Treasurer,

and Attorney-General, of Senators and Representatives, of sheriffs for the several counties, and of justices of the peace for the several towns, and the wards of the city of Providence, shall take place on the Monday aforesaid.

7. The electors of the several towns and wards are authorized to assemble on the day aforesaid, without being notified, as is provided in section 9th of article 10, and without the registration required in section 7th of article 2, and to choose moderators and clerks, and proceed in the election of the officers named in the preceding section.

8. The votes given at the first election for Representatives to the General Assembly, and for justices of the peace, shall be counted by the moderators and clerks of the towns and wards chosen as aforesaid; and certificates of election shall be furnished by them to the Representatives and justices of the peace elected.

9. Said moderators and clerks shall seal up, certify, and transmit to the House of Representatives all the votes that may be given in at said first election for Governor and State officers, and for Senators and sheriffs; and the votes shall be counted as the House of Representatives may direct.

10. The Speaker of the House of Representatives shall, at the first session of the same, qualify himself to administer the oath of office to the members of the House, and to other officers, by taking and subscribing the same oath in the presence of the House.

11. The first session of the General Assembly shall be held in the city of Providence on the first Tuesday of May, in the year one thousand eight hundred and forty-two, with such adjournments as may be necessary; but all other sessions shall be held as is provided in article 4 of this constitution.

12. If any of the Representatives, whom the towns or district are entitled to choose at the first annual election aforesaid, shall not be then elected, or if their places shall become vacant during the year, the same proceedings may be had to complete the election, or to supply vacancies, as are directed concerning elections in the preceding sections of this article.

13. If there shall be no election of Governor or Lieutenant-Governor, or of both of these officers, or of a Senator or Senators, at the first annual election, the House of Representatives, and as many Senators as are chosen, shall forthwith elect, in joint committee, a Governor or Lieutenant-Governor,

or both, or a Senator or Senators, to hold their offices for the remainder of the political year; and, in the case of the two officers first named, until their successors shall be duly qualified.

14. If the number of the justices of the peace determined by the several towns and wards on the day of the first annual election shall not be then chosen, or if vacancies shall occur, the same proceedings shall be had as are provided for in this article in the case of a non-election of Representatives and Senators, or of vacancies in their offices. The justices of the peace thus elected shall hold office for the remainder of the political year, or until the second annual election of justices of the peace, to be held on such day as may be prescribed by the General Assembly.

15. The justices of the peace elected in pursuance of the provisions of this article, may be engaged by the persons acting as moderators of the town and ward meetings, as herein provided; and said justices, after obtaining their certificates of election, may discharge the duties of their office, for a time not exceeding twenty days, without a commission from the Governor.

16. Nothing contained in this article, inconsistent with any of the provisions of other articles of the constitution, shall continue in force for a longer period than the first political year under the same.

17. The present government shall exercise all the powers with which it is now clothed, until the said first Tuesday of May, one thousand eight hundred and forty-two, and until their successors, under this constitution, shall be duly elected and qualified.

18. All civil, judicial, and military officers now elected, or who shall hereafter be elected by the General Assembly, or other competent authority, before the said first Tuesday of May, shall hold their offices, and may exercise their powers, until that time.

19. All laws and statutes, public and private, now in force, and not repugnant to this constitution, shall continue in force until they expire by their own limitation, or are repealed by the General Assembly. All contracts, judgments, actions, and rights of action, shall be as valid as if this constitution had not been made. All debts contracted, and engagements entered into, before the adoption of this constitution, shall be as valid against the State as if this constitution had not been made.

20. The supreme court, established by this constitution, shall have the same jurisdiction as the supreme judicial court at present established; and shall have jurisdiction of all causes which may be appealed to, or pending in the same; and shall be held at the same times and places in each county, as the present supreme judicial court, until the General Assembly shall otherwise prescribe.

21. The citizens of the town of New Shoreham shall be hereafter exempted from military duty, and the duty of serving as jurors in the courts of this State. The citizens of Jamestown shall be forever hereafter exempted from military field duty.

22. The General Assembly shall, at their first session after the adoption of this constitution, propose to the electors the question, whether the word "white," in the first line of the first section of article 2 of the constitution, shall be stricken out. The question shall be voted upon at the succeeding annual election; and if a majority of the electors voting shall vote to strike out the word aforesaid, it shall be stricken from the constitution; otherwise not. If the word aforesaid shall be stricken out, section 3d of article 2 shall cease to be a part of this constitution.

23. The President, Vice-Presidents, and Secretaries shall certify and sign this constitution, and cause the same to be published.

Done in convention, at Providence, on the 18th day of November, in the year one thousand eight hundred and forty-one, and of American independence the sixty-sixth.

JOSEPH JOSLIN, *President of the Convention.*

WAGER WEEDEN,
SAMUEL H. WALES, } *Vice-Presidents.*

Attest:

WILLIAM H. SMITH,
JOHN S. HARRIS, } *Secretaries.*

THE FREEMEN'S CONSTITUTION - 1842

In response to the actions of the unauthorized convention which drew up The People's Constitution and the subsequent ratification by the people, the state legislature drew up this Freemen's Constitution. The residents of the state rejected this document. Subsequently the people reacted by following Thomas Dorr in a rebellion.

Source: Arthur May Mowry. *The Dorr War*. Providence, R. I.: Preston & Rounds Co., 1901, 347-366.

We, the people of the State of Rhode Island and Providence Plantations, do ordain and establish this constitution for the government thereof.

ARTICLE I.

Declaration of Certain Constitutional Rights and Principles.

In order effectually to secure the religious and political freedom established here by our venerated ancestors, and to preserve the same for their posterity, we do declare that the inherent, essential, and unquestionable rights and principles hereinafter mentioned, among others, shall be established, maintained, and preserved, and shall be of paramount obligation in all legislative, judicial, and executive proceedings.

SECTION 1. Every person within this State ought to find a certain remedy, by having recourse to the laws, for all injuries or wrongs which he may receive in his person, property, or character. He ought to obtain right and justice freely and without being obliged to purchase it, completely and without denial, promptly and without delay, conformably to the laws.

SEC. 2. The right of the people to be secure in their persons, papers, and possessions, against unreasonable searches and seizures, shall not be violated; and no warrant shall issue, but on complaint in writing, upon probable cause, supported by oath or affirmation, and describing, as nearly as may be, the place to be searched, and the persons or things to be seized.

THE DORR WAR.

SEC. 3. No person shall be holden to answer for a capital or other infamous crime, unless on presentment or indictment by a grand jury, except in cases of impeachment, or such offences as are usually cognizable by a justice of the peace; or, in cases arising in the land or naval forces, or in the militia, when in actual service, in time of war or public danger. No persons shall be tried after an acquittal, for the same offence.

SEC. 4. Excessive bail shall not be required, nor excessive fines imposed, nor cruel punishments inflicted; and all punishments ought to be proportioned to the offence.

SEC. 5. All persons imprisoned ought to be bailable by sufficient sureties, unless for capital offences, when the proof is evident, or the presumption great. The privilege of the writ of *habeas corpus* shall not be suspended, unless when, in cases of rebellion or invasion, the public safety shall require it; nor ever, without the authority of the General Assembly.

SEC. 6. In all criminal prosecutions, the accused shall enjoy the privilege of a speedy and public trial, by an impartial jury; to be informed of the nature and cause of the accusation; to be confronted with the witnesses against him; to have compulsory process for obtaining them in his favor; and to have the assistance of counsel in his defence, and be at liberty to speak for himself; nor shall he be deprived of life, liberty, or property, unless by the judgment of his peers, or the law of the land.

SEC. 7. The person of a debtor, where there is not strong presumption of fraud, ought not to be continued in prison after he shall have delivered up his property for the benefit of his creditors, in such manner as shall be prescribed by law.

SEC. 8. No *ex post facto* law, or law impairing the obligation of contracts, shall be made.

SEC. 9. No man, in a court of common law, shall be compelled to give evidence criminating himself.

SEC. 10. Every man being presumed innocent until pronounced guilty by the law, all acts of severity that are not necessary to secure an accused person shall be repressed.

SEC. 11. The right of trial by jury shall remain inviolate.

SEC. 12. Private property shall not be taken for public uses, without just compensation.

SEC. 13. The citizens shall continue to enjoy and freely exercise the rights of fishery, and all other rights to which they have heretofore been entitled under the charter of this State, except as is herein otherwise provided.

SEC. 14. The military shall always be held in strict subordination to the civil authority.

SEC. 15. No soldier shall, in time of peace, be quartered in any house, without the consent of the owner; nor in time of war, but in manner to be prescribed by law.

SEC. 16. The liberty of the press being essential to the security of freedom in a State, any person may publish his sentiments on any subject, being responsible for the abuse of that liberty; and in all trials for libel, both civil and criminal, the truth, unless published from malicious motives, shall be a sufficient defence to the person charged.

SEC. 17. The citizens have a right, in a peaceable manner, to assemble for their common good, and to apply to those invested with the powers of government for redress of grievances, or other purposes, by petition, address, or remonstrance.

SEC. 18. The right of the people to keep and bear arms shall not be infringed.

SEC. 19. Slavery shall not be tolerated in this State.

SEC. 20. Whereas Almighty God hath created the mind free, and all attempts to influence it, by temporal punishments or burdens, or by civil incapacitations, tend to beget habits of hypocrisy and meanness; and whereas a principal object of our venerable ancestors, in their migrations to this country, and their settlement of this State, was, as they expressed it, to hold forth a lively experiment, that a flourishing civil State may stand, and be best maintained, with full liberty in religious concernments; we, therefore, declare that no man shall be compelled to frequent or support any religious worship, place, or ministry whatever; nor enforced, restrained, molested, or burdened in his body or goods, nor disqualified from holding any office, nor otherwise suffer, on account of his religious belief; and that all men shall be free to profess, and by argument to maintain, their opinion in matters of religion; and that the same shall in nowise diminish, enlarge, or affect their civil capacities.

SEC. 21. The enumeration of the foregoing rights shall not be construed to impair or deny others retained by the people.

ARTICLE II.

Of the Right of Suffrage.

SECTION 1. Every person who is now a freeman, and qualified voter, shall continue to be so, so long as he retains the qualifications upon which he was admitted.

SEC. 2. Hereafter, every white male native citizen of the United States, or any territory thereof, of the full age of twenty-one years, who shall have had his actual permanent residence and home in this State for the period of one year, and in the town or city in which he may claim a right to vote six months next preceding the time of voting, and shall be seized in his own right of a freehold real estate in such town or city, of the value at least of one hundred and thirty-four dollars over and above all incumbrances, shall, therefrom, have the right to vote in the election of all civil officers, and on all questions in all legal town or ward meetings.

SEC. 3. Every white male native citizen of the United States or any territory thereof, of the full age of twenty-one years, who shall have had his actual permanent residence and home in this State for the period of two years, and in the town or city in which he may claim the right to vote six months next preceding the time of voting, shall have the right to vote in the election of all civil officers, and on all questions in all legal town or ward meetings: *Provided, however*, That no person who is not now a freeman shall be allowed to vote upon any motion to impose a tax, or incur expenditures in any town or city, unless he possess the freehold qualification required by this article, or shall have been taxed upon property valued at least at one hundred and fifty dollars, within one year from the time he may offer to vote, and shall have paid such tax in said town or city.

SEC. 4. Any white male, native of any foreign country, of the full age of twenty-one years, naturalized in the United States according to law, who shall have had his actual permanent residence and home in this State for the period of three years after his naturalization, and in the town or city in which he may claim the right to vote six months next preceding the time of voting, and shall be seized in his own right of a freehold real estate, in such town or city, of the value at least of one hundred and thirty-four dollars over and above all incumbrances, shall, therefrom, have a right to vote in the election of all civil officers, and in all questions in all town or ward meetings. But no person in the military, naval, marine, or any other service of the United States, shall be considered as having the required residence by reason of being employed in any garrison, barrack, or military or naval Station in this State. And no pauper, lunatic, or person *non compos mentis*, or under guardianship, shall be permitted to vote; nor shall any person convicted of any crime deemed infamous at common law, be permitted to exercise that privilege until he be restored thereto by the General Assembly. Persons residing on land ceded by this State to the United States shall not be entitled to exercise the privilege of electors during such residence.

SEC. 5. The General Assembly shall, as soon as may be after the adoption of this constitution, provide for the registration of voters; and shall also have full power generally to enact all laws necessary to carry this article into effect, and to prevent abuse and fraud in voting.

SEC. 6. All persons entitled to vote shall be protected from arrest in civil cases, on the days of election, and on the day preceding and the day following an election.

SEC. 7. In the city of Providence, and all other cities, no person shall be eligible to the office of mayor, alderman, or common councilman, who is not qualified to vote upon a motion to impose a tax or incur expenditures as herein provided.

SEC. 8. The General Assembly shall have power to provide, by special or general laws, for the admission of any native male citizen of the United States, or any territory, who shall have had his permanent residence and home in this State for two years, but who is not otherwise qualified under this article, to vote on such conditions as they may deem proper, except for taxes and expenditures.

ARTICLE III.

Of the Distribution of Powers.

The powers of the government shall be distributed into three distinct branches — the legislative, executive, and judicial.

ARTICLE IV.

Of the Legislative Power.

SECTION 1. This constitution shall be the supreme law of the State; and all laws inconsistent therewith shall be void. The General Assembly shall pass all such laws as are necessary to carry this constitution into effect.

SEC. 2. The legislative power, under this constitution, shall be vested in two distinct houses, or branches, each of which shall have a negative on the other: the one to be styled the Senate, the other the House of Representatives; and both together, the General Assembly. The style of their laws shall be: It is enacted by the General Assembly as follows.

SEC. 3. There shall be one session of the General Assembly holden annually at Newport, on the first Tuesday of May; and one other annual session, to be holden on the last Monday of October, once in two years, at South Kingstown; and the intermediate years, alternately at Bristol and East Greenwich; and the adjournment from the October session shall be holden at Providence.

SEC. 4. No member of the General Assembly shall take any fees, or be of counsel in any case pending before either branch of the General Assembly, under penalty of forfeiting his seat, upon due proof thereof to the satisfaction of the branch of which he is a member.

SEC. 5. The person and estate of every member of the General Assembly shall be free and exempt from any process in any civil action during the session of the General Assembly, and for two days before the commencement and after the termination thereof. And all processes served contrary hereto shall be void. And for any speech in debate, in either House, no member shall be questioned in any other place.

SEC. 6. Each House shall be the judge of the elections and qualifications of its members; and a majority shall constitute a quorum to do business;

but a smaller number may adjourn from day to day, and may compel the attendance of absent members, in such manner, and under such penalties, as each House may prescribe.

SEC. 7. Each House may determine the rules of proceeding, punish contempts, punish its members for disorderly behavior, and, with the concurrence of two-thirds, expel a member; but not a second time for the same cause.

SEC. 8. Each House shall keep a journal of its proceedings. The yeas and nays of the members of either House shall, at the desire of one-fifth of those present, be entered on the journal.

SEC. 9. Neither House shall, during a session, without the consent of the other, adjourn for more than two days, nor to any other place than that in which they may be sitting.

SEC. 10. The General Assembly shall continue to exercise the judicial power, the power of visiting corporations, and all other powers they have heretofore exercised, not inconsistent with this constitution.

SEC. 11. The General Assembly shall regulate the compensation of the Governor and other officers elected by general ticket, or by the General Assembly, and of the members of the General Assembly, subject to the limitations contained in this constitution.

SEC. 12. All lotteries shall hereafter be prohibited in this State, except those already authorized by the General Assembly.

SEC. 13. The General Assembly shall have no power, hereafter, to incur State debts to an amount exceeding fifty thousand dollars, except in time of war, or on case of invasion, without the express consent of the people; nor in any case, without such consent, to pledge the faith of the State for the payment of the obligations of others. This section shall not be construed to refer to any money that may be deposited with this State by the government of the United States.

SEC. 14. The assent of two-thirds of the members elected to each branch of the General Assembly shall be required to every bill appropriating the public moneys, or property, for local or private purposes.

SEC. 15. The General Assembly shall, from time to time, provide for making new valuations of property, for the assessment of taxes, in such manner as they may deem best. No direct State tax shall be assessed upon the ratable property of the State, before a new estimate of such property be taken.

Sec. 16. Whenever a direct tax is laid by the State, one-sixth part thereof shall be assessed on the polls of the qualified electors: provided that the tax on a poll shall never, in any one tax, exceed the sum of fifty cents.

Sec. 17. The General Assembly may provide by law for the continuance in office of any officers of annual appointment, until other persons are qualified to take their places.

ARTICLE V.

Of the House of Representatives.

Section 1. The House of Representatives shall consist of members elected by the electors of the several towns and cities in the respective town and ward meetings. Each town or city having four thousand inhabitants, and under six thousand five hundred, shall be entitled to elect three Representatives; each town or city having six thousand five hundred inhabitants, and under ten thousand, shall be entitled to elect four Representatives; each town or city having ten thousand inhabitants, and under fourteen thousand, shall be entitled to elect five Representatives; each town or city having fourteen thousand inhabitants, and under eighteen thousand, shall be entitled to elect six Representatives; each town or city having eighteen thousand inhabitants, and under twenty-two thousand, shall be entitled to elect seven Representatives; each town or city having over twenty-two thousand inhabitants shall be entitled to elect eight Representatives. But no town or city shall be entitled to elect more than eight Representatives, and every town or city shall be entitled to elect two. The representation of the several towns and cities in this State shall be apportioned agreeable to the last census of the people of the United States preceding the election.

Sec. 2. The House of Representatives shall have authority to elect its Speaker, clerks, and other officers. The oath of office shall be administered by the Secretary of State, or, in his absence, by the Attorney-General. The clerks shall be engaged by the Speaker.

Sec. 3. Whenever the seat of a member of the House of Representatives shall be vacated by death, resignation, or otherwise, the vacancy may be filled by a new election.

SEC. 4. The senior member from the town of Newport, present, shall preside at the organization of the House.

ARTICLE VI.

Of the Senate.

SECTION 1. The Senate shall consist of nineteen members, to be chosen annually by the majority of electors, by districts. The State shall be divided into sixteen districts, as follows:

First. The town of Newport shall constitute the first senatorial district, and shall be entitled to elect two Senators.

Second. The towns of Portsmouth, Middletown, Tiverton, Little Compton, New Shoreham, and Jamestown shall constitute the second senatorial district, and shall be entitled to elect two Senators.

Third. The city of Providence shall constitute the third senatorial district, and shall be entitled to elect two Senators.

Fourth. The town of Smithfield shall constitute the fourth senatorial district, and shall be entitled to elect one Senator.

Fifth. The towns of Cumberland and North Providence shall constitute the fifth senatorial district, and shall be entitled to elect one Senator.

Sixth. The towns of Scituate, Cranston, and Johnston shall constitute the sixth senatorial district, and shall be entitled to one Senator.

Seventh. The towns of Glocester, Foster, and Burrillville shall constitute the seventh senatorial district, and shall be entitled to elect one Senator.

Eighth. The town of South Kingstown shall constitute the eighth senatorial district, and shall be entitled to elect one Senator.

Ninth. The towns of Westerly and Charlestown shall constitute the ninth senatorial district, and shall be entitled to elect one Senator.

Tenth. The towns of Hopkinton and Richmond shall constitute the tenth senatorial district, and shall be entitled to elect one Senator.

Eleventh. The towns of North Kingstown and Exeter shall constitute the eleventh senatorial district, and shall be entitled to elect one Senator.

Twelfth. The town of Bristol shall constitute the twelfth senatorial district, and shall be entitled to elect one Senator.

Thirteenth. The towns of Warren and Barrington shall constitute the thirteenth senatorial district, and shall be entitled to elect one Senator.

Fourteenth. The towns of East Greenwich and West Greenwich shall constitute the fourteenth senatorial district, and shall be entitled to elect one Senator.

Fifteenth. The town of Coventry shall constitute the fifteenth senatorial district, and shall be entitled to elect one Senator.

Sixteenth. The town of Warwick shall constitute the sixteenth senatorial district, and shall be entitled to elect one Senator.

And no more than one Senator shall be elected from any town for the same term, in the second senatorial district.

SEC. 2. The Lieutenant-Governor shall *ex-officio* be a member of the Senate.

The Secretary of State shall be, by virtue of his office, Secretary of the Senate, unless otherwise provided by law; and the Senate may elect such other officers as they may deem necessary.

SEC. 3. If, by reason of death, resignation, or absence, there be no Governor or Lieutenant-Governor present, to preside in the Senate, the Senate shall elect one of their own number to preside, until the Governor or Lieutenant-Governor returns, or until one of said offices is filled according to this constitution; and, until such election is made by the Senate, the Secretary of State shall preside.

ARTICLE VII.

Of Impeachments.

SECTION 1. The House of Representatives shall have the sole power of impeachment.

SEC. 2. All impeachments shall be tried by the Senate; and when sitting for that purpose, they shall be under oath or affirmation. No person shall be convicted, except by vote of two-thirds of the members elected. When the Governor is impeached, the chief or presiding justice of the supreme judicial court for the time being, shall preside, with a casting vote in all preliminary questions.

SEC. 3. The Governor, and all other executive and judicial officers, shall be liable to impeachment; but judgment in such cases shall not extend further than to removal from office. The party convicted shall, nevertheless, be liable to indictment, trial and punishment, according to law.

ARTICLE VIII.

Of the Executive Power.

SECTION 1. The chief executive power of this State shall be vested in a Governor.

SEC. 2. The Governor shall take care that the laws be faithfully executed.

SEC. 3. He shall be captain-general and commander-in-chief of the military and naval forces of this State, except when they shall be called into the service of the United States.

SEC. 4. He shall have power to grant reprieves, after conviction, in all cases, except those of impeachment, until the end of the next session of the General Assembly, and no longer.

SEC. 5. The person filling the office of Governor shall preside in the Senate, and in grand committee; and shall have a right, in case of equal division, to vote; not otherwise.

SEC. 6. He may fill vacancies in office not otherwise provided for by this constitution, or by law, until the same shall be filled by the General Assembly, or the people.

SEC. 7. In case of disagreement between the two Houses of the General Assembly, respecting the time or place of adjournment, certified to him by either, he may adjourn them to such time and place as he shall think proper; provided that the time of adjournment shall not be extended beyond the day of the next stated session.

SEC. 8. He may, on special emergencies, convene the General Assembly at any town in this State, at any time not provided for by law; and in case of danger from the prevalence of epidemic or contagious diseases in either of the places in which the General Assembly may by law meet, or to which they may have been adjourned, or from other circumstances, he may, by proclamation, convene said Assembly at any other place within this State.

Sec. 9. All commissions shall be in the name and by the authority of the State of Rhode Island and Providence Plantations, shall be sealed with the State seal, signed by the Governor, and attested by the Secretary.

Sec. 10. In case of the death, resignation, refusal or inability to serve, or removal from office of the Governor, or of his impeachment or absence from the State, the Lieutenant-Governor shall exercise the powers and authority appertaining to the office of Governor, until another shall be chosen at the next annual election for Governor, and be duly qualified, or until the Governor, impeached or absent, shall be acquitted or return.

Sec. 11. If the offices of Governor and Lieutenant-Governor be both vacant by reason of death, resignation, absence or otherwise, the person entitled to preside over the Senate for the time being shall, in like manner, administer the government until he be superseded by a Governor or Lieutenant-Governor.

Sec. 12. The compensation of the Governor and Lieutenant-Governor shall be established by law, and shall not be diminished during the term for which they were elected.

Sec. 13. The duties and powers of the Secretary, Attorney-General, and General Treasurer shall be the same under this constitution as are now established, or from time to time may be prescribed by law.

ARTICLE IX.

Of Elections.

Section 1. The Governor, Lieutenant-Governor, Senators, Representatives, Secretary of State, Attorney-General, and General Treasurer shall be elected at the town, city, or ward meetings, to be holden on the third Wednesday of April, annually; and shall severally hold their offices for one year, from the first Tuesday in May next succeeding their election, and until others are legally chosen and duly qualified to fill their places.

Sec. 2. The voting for all officers chosen by the people, except town or city officers, shall be by ballot, in manner to be regulated by law. Town or city officers shall be chosen by ballot, on demand of any two persons entitled to vote for the same.

SEC. 3. The names of the persons voted for as Governor, Lieutenant-Governor, Secretary of State, General Treasurer, and Attorney-General shall be put upon one ticket, and the tickets shall be deposited by the moderator or warden in a box by themselves. The names of the persons voted for as Senators and as Representatives shall be put upon separate tickets, and the tickets shall be deposited by the moderator or warden in separate boxes. The polls for all the officers named in this section shall be opened at the same time.

SEC. 4. All the votes given for Governor, Lieutenant-Governor, Secretary of State, General Treasurer, and Attorney-General, and also for Senators, shall remain in the ballot-boxes till the polls are closed. These votes shall then, in open town and ward meetings, be taken out and sealed in separate envelopes by the moderators and town clerks, and by the wardens and ward clerks, who shall certify the same, and forthwith deliver or send them to the Secretary of State; whose duty it shall be securely to keep the same, and to deliver the votes for general officers to the Speaker of the House of Representatives, after the House shall be organized, at the May session of the General Assembly. The votes last named shall without delay be opened, counted, and declared, in such manner as the House of Representatives shall direct. The votes for Senators shall be counted by the Governor and Secretary of State, within seven days from the day of election, and the Governor shall give certificates to the Senators who are elected.

SEC. 5. The votes for Representatives in the several towns, after the polls are declared to be closed for the same, shall be counted by the moderators and clerks, who shall announce the result, and give certificates to the persons elected. If there be no election, or not an election of the whole number of Representatives to which the town is entitled, the polls for Representatives may be re-opened, and the like proceedings shall be had until an election shall take place: provided, however, that an adjournment or adjournments of the election may be made to a time not exceeding seven days from the first meeting.

SEC. 6. In the city of Providence and other cities, the polls for Representatives shall be kept open during the whole time of voting for the day, and the votes in the several wards shall be sealed up at the close of the meeting by the wardens and the ward clerks in open ward meeting, and delivered to the city clerk. The mayor and aldermen of said city or cities shall proceed to count said votes within two days from the day of election; and if no election, or an election of only a portion of the Representatives, shall have taken place, the mayor and aldermen shall order a new election to be held, not more than ten days from the day of the first election, and so on till the election of Representatives shall be completed. Certificates of election shall be furnished by the city clerks to the persons chosen.

SEC. 7. If no person shall have a majority of votes for the office of Governor or Lieutenant-Governor, the Senate and House of Representatives, in grand committee, may choose one by ballot from the two persons having the highest number of votes.

SEC. 8. In case an election of the Secretary of State, Attorney-General, or General Treasurer should fail to be made by the electors at their annual election, the vacancy or vacancies shall be filled by the General Assembly, in grand committee, from the two candidates for such office having the greatest number of the votes of the electors. Or, in case of a vacancy in either of said offices from other causes, between the sessions of the General Assembly, the Governor shall appoint some person to fill the same until a successor elected by the General Assembly is qualified to act; and in such case, and also in all other cases of vacancies not otherwise provided for, the General Assembly may fill the same in any manner they may deem proper.

SEC. 9. If there be no choice of a Senator or Senators at the annual election, or if a vacancy in the Senate occur from any other cause, the Governor shall issue his warrant to the town and ward clerks of the several towns and cities in the senatorial district or districts that may have failed to elect, or where such vacancy may have occurred, requiring them to open town or ward meetings for another election, on a day to be by him appointed, not more than fifteen days from the time of issuing such warrant; and, in such election, a plurality of votes shall elect.

SEC. 10. All general officers shall take the following engagement before they act in their respective offices, to wit: You, ———, being by the free vote of the freemen of this State of Rhode Island and Providence Plantations, elected unto the place of ———, do solemnly swear (or affirm) to be true and faithful unto this State, and to support the constitution of this State and of the United States; that you will faithfully and impartially discharge all the duties of your aforesaid office, to the best of your abilities, according to law: so help you God. Or, this affirmation you make and give upon the peril of perjury. And the members of the General Assembly shall take an engagement to the same effect.

SEC. 11. In all elections held by the people under this constitution, a majority of all the electors voting shall be necessary to the choice of the persons voted for, except as is herein otherwise provided.

SEC. 12. The officers now elected in grand committee, except justices of the peace, shall continue to be so elected until otherwise prescribed by law.

SEC. 13. The oath or affirmation shall be administered to the Governor, Lieutenant-Governor, and Senators, by the Speaker of the House of Representatives, in presence of the House, or elsewhere, by a justice of the supreme judicial court. The Secretary of State, Attorney-General, and General Treasurer, shall be engaged by the person exercising the office of Governor.

ARTICLE X.

Of Qualifications for Office.

SECTION 1. No person shall be qualified to hold the office of Governor, Lieutenant-Governor, Senator, or Representative in the General Assembly unless he be a duly qualified elector. No person shall be elected a Representative to the General Assembly, or to any town or city office, unless he be a qualified elector, and an inhabitant of the town or city which elects him.

SEC. 2. Every person shall be disqualified from holding any office to which he may have been elected, if he be convicted of having offered, or procured any other person to offer, any bribe to secure his election, or the election of any other person.

SEC. 3. The judges of all the courts, and all other officers, both civil and military, shall be bound by oath or affirmation to support this constitution, and the constitution of the United States.

SEC. 4. No person who holds any office under the government of the

United States, or any other State or foreign country, shall be capable of acting as a general officer, or shall take a seat in the General Assembly, unless, at the time of taking his engagement, he shall have resigned his office under such other government. And if any general officer, Senator, Representative, or judge shall, after his election, accept or hold any office under any other government, he shall not be capable thereafter of acting as a general officer, Senator, Representative, or judge, but the office shall be thereby vacated.

ARTICLE XI.

Of the Judicial Power.

SECTION 1. The judicial power of this State shall be vested in one supreme judicial court, and in such inferior courts as the General Assembly may, from time to time, ordain and establish; and the jurisdiction of the supreme and of all other courts may, from time to time, be regulated by the General Assembly.

SEC. 2. Chancery powers may be conferred by the General Assembly on the supreme judicial court; but no other court exercising chancery powers shall be established in this State, except as is now provided by law.

SEC. 3. The justices of the supreme judicial court shall be elected in grand committee of the two Houses, to hold their offices until their places be declared vacant by a resolution of the General Assembly to that effect, which shall be voted for by a majority of all the members elected to the House in which it may originate, and be concurred in by the same majority of the other House. Such resolution shall not be entertained at any other than the annual session for the election of public officers; and, in default of the passage thereof at said session, the judge, or judges, shall hold his or their places, as is herein provided. But a judge of this, or of any other court inferior to the same, shall be removable from office, if, upon impeachment, he shall be found guilty of any official misdemeanor.

SEC. 4. In case of vacancy by the death, resignation, refusal, or inability to serve, or absence from the State, of a judge of this court, his place may be filled by the grand committee, until the next annual election; when the judge elected shall hold his office as before provided.

SEC. 5. The judges of the supreme judicial court shall receive a suitable compensation for their services, which shall not be diminished during their continuance in office.

SEC. 6. The judges of the supreme judicial court shall, in all trials, instruct the jury in the law.

SEC. 7. There shall be annually elected by each town, and by the several wards in the city of Providence, a sufficient number of justices of the peace, or wardens, resident therein, with such jurisdiction as the General Assembly may prescribe. And said justices, or wardens (except in the towns of New Shoreham and Jamestown), shall be commissioned by the Governor.

SEC. 8. The courts of probate in this State, excepting the supreme judicial court, shall remain as at present established by law, until the General Assembly shall otherwise prescribe.

ARTICLE XII.

Of Education.

SECTION 1. The diffusion of knowledge as well as of virtue among the people being essential for the preservation of their rights and liberties, it shall be the duty of the General Assembly to promote public schools, and to adopt all other means to secure to the people the advantages and opportunities of education, which they may deem necessary and proper.

SEC. 2. The money which now is, or which may hereafter be, appropriated by law for the formation of a permanent fund for the support of public schools, shall be securely invested, and remain a perpetual fund for that purpose.

SEC. 3. All donations for the support of public schools, or for other purposes of education, which shall be received by the General Assembly, shall be applied according to the terms prescribed by the donors.

SEC. 4. The General Assembly shall make all necessary provisions by law for carrying this article into effect. They are prohibited from diverting said moneys or fund from the aforesaid uses; and from borrowing, appropriating, or using the same, or any part thereof, for any other purpose, under any pretence whatsoever.

ARTICLE XIII.

Of Amendments.

The General Assembly may propose amendments to this constitution by the votes of a majority of all the members elected to each House. Such propositions shall be published in the newspapers, and printed copies of such propositions shall be sent by the Secretary of State, with the names of all the members who shall have voted thereon, with the yeas and nays, to all the town and city clerks in the State; and the said propositions shall be by said clerks inserted in the warrants or notices by them issued for warning the next annual ward and town meetings in April; and the clerks shall read such propositions to the electors when thus assembled, with the names of all the Representatives and Senators who shall have voted thereon, with the yeas and nays, before the election of Representatives and Senators shall be had. If a majority of all the members elected to each House, at said annual meeting, shall approve any proposition thus made, the same shall be published and sent to the electors in the mode provided in the act of approval; and, if then approved by three-fifths of the electors of the State present, and voting thereon in town and ward meetings, it shall become a part of the constitution of the State.

ARTICLE XIV.

Of the Adoption of this Constitution.

SECTION 1. This constitution, if adopted, shall go into operation on the first Tuesday of May, in the year one thousand eight hundred and forty-two. The first election of Governor, Lieutenant-Governor, Secretary of State, Attorney-General, and General Treasurer, and of Representatives and Senators, under said constitution, shall be had on the third Wednesday of April preceding. And the town and ward meetings therefor shall be warned and conducted as is now provided by law. All civil, judicial, and military officers now elected, or who shall hereafter be elected, by the General Assembly or other competent authority, before the said first Tuesday of May, shall hold their offices, and may exercise their powers, until that time, or until their successors are qualified to act. All statutes, public and private, not repugnant to this constitution, shall continue in force until they expire by their own limitation, or are repealed by the General Assembly. All charters, contracts, judgments, actions, and rights of action, shall be as valid as if this constitution had not been made. The present government shall exercise all the powers with which it is now clothed until the said first Tuesday of May, one thousand eight hundred and forty-two, and until their successors, under this constitution, are duly elected and qualified.

Sec. 2. All debts contracted, and engagements entered into, before the adoption of this constitution, shall be as valid against the State as if this constitution had not been formed.

Sec. 3. The supreme judicial court, established by this constitution, shall have the same jurisdiction as the supreme judicial court at present established; and shall have jurisdiction of all causes which may be appealed to, or pending in, the same; and shall be held at the same time and places, and in each county, as the present supreme judicial court, until otherwise prescribed by the General Assembly.

Sec. 4. The towns of Jamestown and New Shoreham shall continue to enjoy the exemption from military duty which they now enjoy, until otherwise prescribed by law.

Done in convention, February 19, 1842.

HENRY Y. CRANSTON,
President of the Convention.

Thomas A. Jenckes, *Secretary.*
Walter W. Updike, *Assistant Secretary.*

State of Rhode Island and Providence Plantations,

In Convention, February 19, A. D. 1842.

Resolved, That the constitution framed by this convention be certified by the president and secretaries, and, with the journal and papers of the convention, shall be deposited in the office of the Secretary of State; that the

Secretary of State cause said constitution, together with this resolution, and all the acts and resolutions of the General Assembly relating to this convention, to be printed and distributed according to law; and that said constitution be submitted to all the people authorized to vote for general officers under the same, for their ratification or rejection, at town and ward meetings, to be holden in the several towns and in the city of Providence, on Monday, Tuesday, and Wednesday, the twenty-first, twenty-second, and twenty-third days of March, A. D. 1842. The several town and city clerks shall issue the necessary warrants for said meetings. Said meetings shall be kept open for the reception of votes from the hour of nine o'clock in the forenoon, until seven o'clock in the afternoon; and in the city of Providence and town of Newport, until nine o'clock in the evening, on the days appointed. At said town and ward meetings every person voting shall have his name written on the back of his ballot; and said ballots shall be sealed up in open town or ward meetings, and, with lists of the names of the voters, shall be returned to the General Assembly at their session to be holden on the fourth Monday of March next.

Read and adopted, February 19, 1842.

THOMAS A. JENCKES, *Secretary*.

DORR'S REBELLION IN RHODE ISLAND - 1842

Source: <u>America. Great Crises In Our History Told By Its Makers</u>. Chicago: Issued By Americanization Department, Veterans of Foreign Wars, 1925.

By C. C. Jewett

THOMAS WILSON DORR, celebrated as the leader of the rebellion in Rhode Island which bears his name, succeeded dramatically, in 1842, in procuring an extension of the right of suffrage in the State, although the rebellion failed and Dorr was convicted of treason and sentenced to imprisonment for life. After serving three years, however, he was released and his citizenship was restored.

At that time the Rhode Island form of government was based on the charter issued by Charles II in 1663, and by the act of 1798, the suffrage had been granted only to those who had a freehold valued at $134, or bringing an annual rental of $7. Also Providence, with twenty times the population of Portsmouth, had the same number of representatives in the State Assembly. Prior to the events recorded in the accompanying letter written by a resident of Providence, Dorr had vainly sought Federal support. Though his methods were revolutionary and unwise, they led to the adoption of the present constitution.

ON MONDAY, May 16th, 1842, Thomas W. Dorr, calling himself the Governor of Rhode Island, arrived in Providence, from New York and Washington. He was met at the State line, by a gang of armed men and boys, who accompanied him in an extra train of cars on the Stonington Railroad to the depot in Providence, where he was received by a large collection of people, some armed, some unarmed. He was escorted into the city by a procession numbering about twelve hundred—three hundred of whom were under arms—preceded by a band of music. They paraded through the principal streets, Dorr being seated in an open carriage, with a sword at his side and the bayonets of his followers bristling in the rear, seemed to fancy himself not only Governor, but monarch of all he surveyed. The citizens, for, be it known, that most of those who swelled the throng at his heels, could not claim the honor of belonging to Providence—the citizens, looked on, with teeth set and flashing eyes. I had read but an hour or two before, Dorr's "Proclamation," heralding his approach, in which he declared war not only against Rhode Island but against the government of the United States—saying that though the authorities of Rhode Island and of the United States were against him, the people were everywhere on his side, and that he was ready to make Rhode Island the battle ground of American Liberty. I had watched this whole struggle with intense anxiety. I thought I could see the interests of rational liberty throughout the United States, depending upon the issue. Two days' success of such principles as Dorr advocated would have thrown the whole Union into convulsions. . . .

After parading the streets a few hours and addressing his followers in a most inflammatory speech, Dorr took up his quarters at the house of one Burrington Anthony, formerly United States Marshal for Rhode Island, and Dorr's High Sheriff for the county of Providence. The house is on Federal Hill, a short remove from the thickly settled part of the city. A large company of armed men were retained to guard the house.

At one o'clock, P. M., on Tuesday, Dorr ordered the signal guns for collecting his friends to be fired. They soon came flocking from all quarters. In the afternoon, a company of them came down into the city and carried away, without resistance, two brass six-pounders from the alarm-post of the United Train of Artillery. It was generally supposed in the town that the only object of this gathering was to prevent arrests. But towards night information reached Governor King, from sources that could be relied on, that an attack would be made on the arsenal that very night.

The State officers now moved with an energy and resolution worthy of all praise. A strong additional guard was sent to the arsenal. Notices were immediately printed and circulated through the city, requesting all who were disposed to maintain law and order to repair forthwith to the arsenal and receive arms. A steamboat was dispatched as soon as she could be got ready to bring companies from Warren, Bristol and Newport, and messengers were sent off in advance of the boat to give the alarm. All this occurred about seven o'clock in the evening. I went over to the arsenal to receive my musket, and everything looked warlike. . . . On returning from the arsenal through one of the most populous streets of the city I found that many, walking like myself, with their muskets, were stopped by squads of armed men, who, aided by the darkness, came suddenly upon them and wrenched away their arms. I only avoided a fight for my own by turning into another street and taking a circuitous route. About one thousand stands of arms were distributed among the citizens. But a comparatively small number of these fell into the hands of the rebels.

The system of espionage established through the city was one of the most fearful things of the whole affair. A group of citizens could not assemble at the corner of a street, in a store, or a public building, and scarcely in a private house, but some spy would be standing silently in their midst, listening to all that was said, and taking down the name of any one who expressed an opinion in opposition to the conspirators. . . .

The watchmen of the city, their numbers much increased by volunteers, were all armed, and many of them provided with horses. . . . The signal was agreed upon, and all awaited the event in terrible suspense. At two o'clock in the morning the alarm was sounded. The bells rung violently a few moments, then commenced the alarm toll—three strokes of a bell, answered by three of the next, and that by another, and so on around the city. The moon had set —a heavy fog rested on the river, and brooded over the town. The people began to gather. Every good man felt it his duty to show himself, wives retained not their husbands, Spartan mothers bade their sons go forth. Everyone knew the crisis had come. . . .

One veteran I well remember, who entered the armory, straightening up to the height of his manhood's prime, the fire of youth still burning beneath the white fringers of his wrinkled brows, "Will you take a man who can fight, but can't run?" said he. He was received with a spontaneous burst of applause —almost the only sound above a low, solemn tone, which I heard on that fearful night. . . .

The cause of the alarm was information brought by the watch that the conspirators had left their position and were moving toward the arsenal. At two o'clock in the morning they commenced their march. Their numbers had been variously estimated at from three to eight hundred. There were probably six hundred in all, and one half of them armed. They advanced near to the arsenal and demanded a surrender in the name of Colonel Wheeler, and in behalf of Governor Dorr. The arsenal was commanded by Colonel Leonard Blodget, a fearless man and an excellent officer. His answer was, "I know no such man as Colonel Wheeler, or Governor Dorr."

"Governor Dorr is present and with a sufficient force to batter down and take the arsenal if it is not surrendered. Must I carry back the answer you have given?"

"That or none."

Dorr then ordered the cannon—two six-pounders —to be brought within musket shot. They were heavily charged with ball and slugs. He gave the order to fire. It was followed by no report. He repeated the order with the same result. Suspecting his men of treachery, he became perfectly furious, brandished his sword, and with bitter imprecations seized a match and applied it himself. The powder flashed harmlessly upon the piece. He probably saw the truth, that his own followers would not sustain him in his desperate career; and, filled with rage and chagrin, he withdrew immediately to his old quarters. . . .

While these events were transpiring at the arsenal, the companies from the city were moving towards the scene of action a mile and a half distant. Their march can never be forgotten by any who were present. The stillness of midnight was broken only by the solemn tolls of the bells, the quick footfall of citizen after citizen as he left his home and hurried armed to join the ranks, and the occasional report of a cannon which came booming across the cove from the rebel quarters. The companies moved on, speechless and without music, a dark mass in solid phalanx, amid darkness and gloom, to a fate they knew not, but resolved to meet it like men. . . .

The sudden retreat of Dorr prevented the necessity of immediate conflict. At daylight a notice issued by the Mayor was circulated through the city requesting all men to close their places of business during the day, and to meet at the Cadet alarm-post, at half past seven o'clock. Dorr ordered his men to breakfast and to be at their posts by seven, prepared to defend him to the last. About seven, the steamboat arrived, bringing the Warren, Bristol and Newport troops, a hundred and sixty-one in number—as fine, resolute looking body of men as I ever saw. . . .

Punctual to the hour, the citizens assembled and joined the various military companies, and the whole body, numbering more than five hundred men, with six field-pieces, moved off towards Federal Hill, under command of Governor King and Colonel William Blodget. . . .

As we were approaching Dorr's headquarters, the report came that he had fled—but no one seemed to believe it, it was so unlike what we had been led to expect of him. . . . Governor King, with the High Sheriff, at the head of one of the companies, now entered the house, amid shouts and threats, but without a gun being fired, searched it thoroughly, and announced to the troops that Dorr had actually fled. His flight, it seems, was so secret that only two or three of his own men knew it till a short time before it was thus announced. A company of men on horseback were despatched in pursuit of Dorr, and the attention of the rest directed to taking the cannon from the remaining mob of insurgents, and dispersing them. It seemed impossible to do this without the loss of many valuable lives. They were strongly posted—they were men, ferocious by nature, desperate in circumstances, and infuriated by liquor. They brandished their lighted matches within a few inches of their heavy-loaded cannon, and were several times prevented from firing only by some one of them less drunk, who struck off the match with a sword just as it was descending upon the powder. At this time we were facing their cannon, in a perfectly straight street, within half musket shot. . . .

The Governor exhorted them for the last time to disperse. They answered only with oats and threats, and bravado. He waited a short time, and just as the word was given, the leaders of the rebels entreated the Governor to stop, told him that the men were drunk, and that they themselves had lost all command of them; but that if he would withdraw his forces from the ground, they would pledge themselves to return the cannon, and would induce the men to disperse as soon as the madness from rum had somewhat abated. . . . In consideration of these statements and pledges, and to spare the lives of citizens who might otherwise be slaughtered, the Governor withdrew his forces. But no sooner had they returned to the armories than the miscreants, joined by many others, refused to return the guns and commenced throwing up a breastwork to defend themselves. . . . They worked all night, and drank deeply of rum—but the cold dews and the hard labor, had a wonderful effect in sobering them, so that towards morning finding they were not reinforced as they expected to be, they brought back the cannon and dispersed.

RHODE ISLAND IN 1907

The following is a discussion
of conditions in Rhode Island
and how they have been improving.

Source: <u>New England Magazine</u>, October 1907, 131-160.

WHAT'S THE MATTER WITH NEW ENGLAND?

IV

RHODE ISLAND, THE STATE ON THE UP-GRADE : THE HOME
OF THE HIGH-GRADE IMMIGRANT, OF MIGHTY MANU-
FACTORIES, OF PECULIAR POLITICS, AND AN
EARNEST DESIRE FOR BETTER CONDITIONS

By FRANK PUTNAM

RHODE ISLAND, the smallest and most densely populated State in the Union, covers a thousand square miles of land and three hundred miles of water — about the size of a small county in Texas. The traveller, having these facts in mind, is amazed, as he rides up and down the railways, to see how large a portion of Rhode Island is abandoned to wild pasture and scrub timber. Railroad lines cross the State from east to west through the northern, central, and southern tiers of towns, but more than one-half of its area has no outlet by either steam line or trolley. For example, there is no railway along the southern coast of the State, nor any north and south line traversing the western towns.

The population of the State is 480,000, an increase of nearly twenty-one per cent in ten years. This is much larger than the total increase for the same period in Maine, New Hampshire, and Vermont. Of the 480,000, Colonel Webb, the State's commissioner of industrial statistics, tells me 248,000, according to a census he has just completed, are Roman Catholic, and about thirty-five per cent are of foreign birth. Sixty-five per cent of the State's population are either of foreign birth or parentage. Most of the immigrants came in from Ireland, French Canada, and, latterly, from Italy. The Irish are mainly Democratic in politics; the French as a rule are Republican; and the Italians also show a tendency to join the Republican party. Taken altogether, they fit rapidly and well into the intense and complicated industrial and political life of the commonwealth. Indeed, it is the boast of Rhode Island that she gets the pick of the skilled workmen that come to America from foreign lands. She has no port of entry for immigrants, but the fame of her great mills and factories, which are not only in many instances the largest but also the most perfect of their kind in America, attracts the skilled and intelligent new-comer and so maintains the high standard of her industrial institutions.

Almost as Many Shops as Farms

Less than one-eighth of Rhode Island's population is engaged in farming. There are between five thousand and six thousand farms in operation, and almost an equal number of shops and factories devoted to manufacturing and repairing. More than any other State, Rhode Island carries all her eggs in one basket, and fulfils Pudd'nhead Wilson's rule for success by keeping her eyes constantly upon that basket. Manufacturing is the chief and almost the sole business of the people of Little Rhody. There are nearly two thousand shops and factories that have an annual turn-over of more than $500 each — or one for each 250 inhabitants.

On the farms the chief crop is hay, which finds a good market in the manufacturing centres where many horses are kept. There is very little market-gardening done. This industry is increasing somewhat in the neighborhood of the larger cities,— Providence, Pawtucket, Newport, and Woonsocket,— but most of the cities' supply of fresh vegetables is brought in from the South. Doubtless, now that the Italians are turning their attention to this work, they will in due season bring it up the same high and very profitable development that they have achieved in the market-gardening districts tributary to Boston.

The State maintains an agricultural college at Kingston, and supports it liberally, considering the small extent of the industry; but the manufacturing industries, with their better opportunities for exceptional talent, steadily draw the most enterprising youths from the farms into the cities. As a not unnatural consequence, many of the farming-towns have long been at a standstill in population and development. Some of them have fewer inhabitants than they had fifty years ago. Religion, education, and the social virtues and graces that flow out of these influences have declined with the decline of agriculture and the churches and schools that it once supported.

Rural Towns Need Rail Outlets

But the State is unmistakably on the upgrade in every way, and this advance movement is shared to some extent by even the most backward of the country towns. They suffer most from the lack of means of getting their products into the city markets. There is no doubt that if either the State or private companies were to build and operate electric trolley-lines connecting the remoter country towns with the urban centres, the resultant gains, both in money and character, would amply make good the investment. Much of the land that now lies idle, or that is worked in a hopeless fashion, is capable, I am assured on good authority, of being made profitably productive if means are afforded to get its products into the city markets. If private capital continues indifferent to the opportunity here presented the State might well take up the work. Its investment should be made good by the resultant increase in taxable values alone, to say nothing of the upward impulse that would be given to the population of those towns now contemptuously and somewhat unjustly dubbed "barbarian" by their more fortunate neighbors in the thriving urban communities.

This subject is one that should command the attention of the Legislature. At present, for causes that will be explained further on, the country towns dominate the Legislature; but the trend is toward a readjustment of representation that will lodge control in the hands of the cities. If the country towns are wise, they will make use of their power while they still have it to provide the obviously needed means of developing their resources. The Legislature might either appropriate State funds to build electric lines through the towns that are now shut out from the world by lack of them, these lines to be operated by the State or leased to private companies, or it might grant franchises to private companies upon terms sufficiently favorable to induce the investment of capital that would otherwise hold aloof from this field.

Big Industries Built by Brains and Energy

The manufactures of Rhode Island, like those of Vermont, represent brains and energy far more than any natural advantages. The State has neither coal nor iron. It is served by a single railroad, the New York, New Haven & Hartford, and it has no good seaport. Providence is located a dozen miles above deep water, on Narragansett Bay, and is only a barge port. A few coasting-vessels of light draught enter the port, but deep-sea-going vessels cannot come in there. The city owns no docks, and the private wharves are so few that sea-traffic languishes. During the coal strike vessels had frequently to wait several days for a chance to unload their cargoes. General Brayton told me that it was originally intended to locate the city a dozen miles further down the bay. The land was platted and plans made, but in the curious ways often taken by city growth, the trend was up the bay and away from the sea.

I asked General Brayton, who for thirty years, by common report, has "bossed" the political affairs of Rhode Island, and who probably knows the State as well as any other living man, why Rhode Island's representatives in Congress had never got federal appropriations to give Providence the first-class harbor to which her size and commerce entitle her. It seemed to me that Providence, situated two hundred miles nearer the South than Boston, ought to have become the principal sea-gate of New England. General Brayton explained that for a dozen miles below the city Narragansett Bay is shallow, and that in order to maintain a good channel it would be necessary to dredge constantly, at large expense. He did not tell me that the railroad, whose chief legislative representative he is, receiving a large annual salary, had subtly opposed harbor improvements; but, remembering how the transcontinental lines have always, openly and secretly, fought the Panama Canal project, I wondered whether Providence's lack of harbor facilities might not be due to the quiet manipulation of the railroad. The government has to dredge constantly in the harbors of New York, Galveston, New Orleans, and other great ports, and its original outlay for harbors in these and other cities has been greater than it would need be at Providence. It seemed to me that Senator Aldrich, the most powerful member of the United States Senate, could have got for Providence at least equal favor with New Orleans, Galveston, and Houston. "But we have only two representatives in the House," said General Brayton. The explanation seems scarcely sufficient.

Rhode Island would certainly profit largely by procuring a deep harbor and adequate wharfage at Providence, and by rail communication between her isolated farming-towns and her cities. Perhaps these are the most important opportunities which now seem to be neglected in the State's industrial program.

Factory Villages in the Country

You ride along on any of the railway lines in the State, through long stretches of wild lands, unused and almost uninhabited, until suddenly you come into a pretty mill village situated on a river. There are many of these communities, located in rural environment but having practically no connection with rural life. If you are from the South, or the Middle West, you will wonder, perhaps, at the high fences with locked gates that enclose the big textile mills. This custom of locking workmen in, and locking the rest of the world out, adapted from the textile districts of the Old World, has not yet found its way West or South to any extent. You will see a few of these mill barricades in Georgia and the Carolinas, where the New Englanders have taken hold of the industry, but it jars upon one bred in the States further West. There, except in a very few of the largest cities, and in a few big trust factories only, the workmen are not restrained by high fences and locked gates. It used to be said, not so many years ago, that when a Chicago man wanted to put livery on his servants he had to send East to get the servants; no Western man would wear livery. There was something in the atmosphere that made it seem a degradation, and the West would probably regard the locked gates and the factory high fences in much the same way that it regards the wearing of livery.

On the other hand, there has been little in the West and South of that development of benevolent paternalism, expressed in what is called welfare work among factory hands, that is common in Rhode Island. Many of the larger manufacturing companies, in woollens, cotton, and metals, have gone far beyond the letter of the State's requirements in providing clean and comfortable shops, and in assisting their employees to broaden and brighten their social life. Perhaps one of the chief factors in the success of Rhode Island's manufactures, aside from the inventive and constructive genius of the men that built them up, has been the employers' intelligent recognition of the fact that the most profitable employee is a contented one. Doubtless this general policy explains, also, the tendency of the most intelligent mechanics coming here from abroad to seek employment in Rhode Island.

Wages in the factories of Rhode Island compare favorably with those in like lines in the rest of New England. They are not high, as compared with wages in the West, but the West has few cotton or woollen mills, and none comparable in size with those of New England. As for the cotton-mills in the South, labor conditions there are far worse than in New England, as a rule.

The State Is Very Prosperous

Considered as a whole, the manufactures of Rhode Island show a slow but constant tendency toward the reduction of hours of labor and increased wages. The State is highly prosperous, especially at the top. It has developed a very large number of huge private fortunes, and its wage-earners hold in the aggregate a very large amount of savings. Indeed, it may truthfully be said that the three great trust companies that dominate Rhode Island's financial affairs — the Industrial, the Union, and the Rhode Island Hospital trusts — have been built upon the small savings of the wage-earners quite as much as upon the accumulated surplus of the mill and factory proprietors.

There has been in Rhode Island even more than in other States a marked tendency toward concentration of industries. The rubber trade is controlled by the United States Rubber Company, the trust; woollen and cotton manufacturing is chiefly in the hands of a few families and corporations; some of these proprietors own and operate many mills in other New England States. For example, Robert Knight, the largest individual owner of cotton-mills in the world, controls over twenty establishments,— many in Rhode Island, some in Massachusetts. But this centralizing tendency has not suppressed individual initiative operating on a small scale. It may have diverted it from the industries centralized, but the fact that Rhode Island has so large a number of small factories of various kinds proves that her people have a high degree of commercial adaptability, and tends to disprove the theory that the trusts must rapidly abolish the middle class of independent small manufacturers and traders. That result may come in time, but it is not yet in sight, in Rhode Island.

Excepting the scattered mills and factories along the rivers, noted above in the comment upon the country towns, Rhode Island's manufactures are highly concentrated in a few cities. Broadly speaking, Greater Providence includes the thriving cities of Pawtucket and Woonsocket, and with these and other near-by manufacturing centres comprises a large majority of the manufactures and the population of the State.

The "Summer Social Capital" of America

Newport, the other considerable city of the State, situated on the inner shore of the island of Rhode Island, is the seat of the richest seaside colony in America. The old town, once a busy centre of commerce with the far East, and still later a great slave mart, has long since ceased to figure in the State's industrial statistics. Huge and sometimes beautiful palaces built by the wealthy families of New York, and occupied by them during the summer season, form a social centre that is sometimes referred to as the summer social capital of the United States. At any rate, it supplies most of that palpitating society gossip with which the newspapers are wont to entertain wide-eyed readers of the less affluent classes. The narrow streets, the statues of the Perrys, and the historical buildings clothe the older portion of the town in a romantic atmosphere of bygone times. This mood in the casual traveller's mind is likely to be rudely jarred by the sudden apparition of a splendid carriage with three gorgeously liveried flunkies perched upon it, or by the passing of a group of brisk and gay young blue-shirted soldiers from one of the near-by forts.

The single railway-station at Newport is a marvel of decrepitude and dirt. It is matched only by the ancient and unspeakably dirty, dusty passenger-cars that are run between Newport and Boston. The only inference the stranger can draw from this railway service into "America's summer social capital" is that the rich come in automobiles and private yachts and the rest don't count with the railroad. At this point it may be set down as a general observation that the railroad-passenger service in old, rich, and thickly settled New England is as a whole decidedly inferior in quality to that of the better Western railroads. There is still some show of competition in the Middle West. Even though one group of New York financiers may control several roads in a given territory, the active managers of these roads have an incentive to competition in the desire to excel each other in the amount of business done. This active rivalry for business may obtain between divisions of the great system which controls southern New England, but it does not show in sumptuous equipment.

The State's Leading Industries

The principal industry of Rhode Island, in the number of people employed and the value of product, is the manufacture of woollen goods. The woollen-mills, including those which make worsteds, employed, according to the last census bulletin, 19,399 people, of whom 9,582 were listed as "men over sixteen years old;" 7,984, as "women over sixteen years;" and 1,833 as children under sixteen years. The capital invested was nearly $47,000,000; the number of establishments, thirty-two; the wages, nearly ten millions; the value of products, a little above $52,500,000. Cotton manufacturing runs a close second to woollens. The value of cotton-mill products in the same year was over $30,000,000, and the wages nearly eight millions. Foundry and machine-shop products rank third in the list, with 9,294 employees, and an annual output worth nearly $16,500,000. Providence is the chief centre of the jewelry trade of the United States. With Attleboro, the near-by city in Massachusetts, it produces more jewelry than any other section of the country. The 6,475 workers employed in the jewelry trade of Rhode Island in 1905, the latest year for which figures are obtainable, earned $3,181,597 in wages and turned out a product worth $14,431,756. The industry of dyeing and finishing textiles is of almost equal prominence, the value of its product reaching close to ten millions on an invested capital of something less than seventeen millions. It employed 7,562 hands. The total of the State's wage-earners in manufactures of all kinds was 98,813, with a total product valued at $184,074,378. It is estimated that there has been a gain of at least five per cent in both figures since the census was taken.

Corruption in Politics

Accepting the theory that bad news travels much faster than good news, we are able to understand how the country at large has heard more about Rhode Island's political corruption than about her remarkable industrial achievements.

It is probable — I have not studied the political systems of *all* the States — that Rhode Island has the most inequitable political system of any Northern commonwealth. The student of conditions in New Hampshire might suppose that State had reached the limit of subserviency to corporate rule of public affairs; but in Rhode Island he would learn of yet further refinements of the game of politics as it is played by the big corporations. Good Rhode Islanders declare that Connecticut is the true "limit." However that may be, Little Rhody is bad enough.

The political bosses of Rhode Island have even refined the art of bribery in elections. Crude amateurs in other States think they have done something worth bragging about when they win an election with purchased votes. In Rhode Island when it is doubted whether enough votes can be bought to insure a desired result, the buyers finish the job by *hiring members of the opposition party to stay away from the polls*. A bought vote, one that would otherwise have been cast against your candidate, counts two points for your man. Hiring a member of the opposition not to vote at all counts only one point for your man. I was assured that there are a good many voters who would scorn an offer of money to sell their votes, but whose consciences permit them to take money for staying away from the polls. The positive sin they will not commit; the negative sin they do not balk at. In the country towns a considerable minority of the citizens have come to feel that some one ought to pay them for the time they lose in going to the polls. They regard voting, not as a precious and sacred privilege, but as a public service for which they are justly entitled to payment from some source.

I have encountered this curiously perverted idea in various parts of New England. It obtains also in Chicago, in New York City, in most of the larger cities, to some extent; but in the rural West it has not yet taken root. The theory that recent immigrants brought this conception of the suffrage over with them, wickedly corrupting the natives, will not hold water. The buying of votes has been a source of scandal in Rhode Island for more than a hundred and fifty years. The late-comers are those who have suffered from contact with this idea. When they come into a new land, they naturally accept its customs to some extent, both the good and the bad. Indeed, in Rhode Island it is notorious that the most flagrant bribery, the most utterly treasonable disregard of the citizen's duty to the State, takes place in the country towns, where the percentage of so-called native stock is very much higher than it is in the cities.

How the State Has Been "For Sale"

Lincoln Steffens two years ago dubbed Rhode Island "A State for sale." That was probably true, in respect of the official machinery of the State. You could not have gone up to the State-house and bought a piece of legislation from the members direct; but you could, it is generally believed, have got your bill passed if you dealt first with General Charles R. Brayton, the king of the lobby enthroned in the office of the high sheriff. You could not have bought the influence of Governor Utter, but you would have had no need to buy it, since the Governor has no veto power, and the Legislature did General Brayton's bidding.

It is of course absurd to say that any one could buy a majority of the voters, in Rhode Island or in any other State. Every man may have his price, but no man or corporation has every man's price. In order to get around this dead wall, politicians frequently so arrange the political machinery of a State that a small amount of bribery will give them control. In Rhode Island the State Senate is the bulwark of the corruptionists, and representation in the lower House is also far from equitable. Each town and city in the State — thirty-eight in all — is entitled to one State senator. Providence, which cast more than 23,000 votes in the last congressional elections, has one senator. So, too, has Little Compton, which cast 135 votes; and Jamestown, which cast 170.

In a word, the four cities, — Providence, Pawtucket, Newport, and Woonsocket, — which cast 38,033 votes in the last congressional elections, have four members of the State Senate, and the thirty-four smaller cities and towns, which cast a total of 27,476 votes at the same election, have thirty-four members of the State Senate.

Where this condition prevails it is obviously easy for a corrupt boss, supported by greedy or cowardly corporations, to control the State. He has no need to win a majority of the voters of the State to keep his party in power. He need only make sure that his legislative candidates are chosen in a majority of the small towns, where but a few votes are cast, and the trick is done. In Rhode Island the boss found ready to his hands a condition admirably suited for his uses. When General Brayton set up business as a lobbyist thirty years ago he found the country towns dwindling and impoverished agriculturally. He found them inhabited chiefly by descendants of the early settlers of the State, jealous of the growing population and influence of the cities which were rapidly filling up with later immigrants. Plainly it was in the interest of General Brayton, and of his clients, the corporations that might need special privileges, to maintain this condition. They have managed to maintain it, but the signs of this day are adverse to them.

Some Signs of Improvement

In the first place, Senator Nelson W. Aldrich, the brains of the Rhode Island Republican machine, has "made his pile," as the phrase goes, and has accordingly lost his most active personal interest in the fight. True, he is still most useful to his allies in the United States Senate, and he has shown no disposition to retire from office; but he more and more leaves the heat of the battle to others. Once in six years, near the expiration of his own term, he comes to Rhode Island and takes personal command of the forces. As Governor Higgins, in terms bitterly contemptuous, said to me, "The chairman of the Finance Committee of the United States Senate, the most august legislative body on earth, comes home once in six years and does not hesitate to sit in a low groggery and deal with political crooks and rumsellers to insure his own reëlection."

In the second place, a considerable minority of the Republicans of Rhode Island have united with the Democrats in a campaign to drive bribe-givers and bribe-takers out of politics. The fusionists nominated Robert H. I. Goddard, one of the mill millionaires of the State, a fellow of Brown University, a soldier of the Civil War with a fine record, and a man of ability, for United States senator to succeed Mr. Wetmore of Newport. Mr. Wetmore was again a candidate, and Colonel Samuel P. Colt, the president of the United States Rubber Company, was a third aspirant. Colonel Goodard led throughout the balloting in the legislative session of 1907, but could not obtain a majority. His friends say that "if he had been willing to buy votes, he could have won in a walk." Colonel Colt had the support of General Brayton and his influences, and was preferred also by Senator Aldrich, though the latter uttered no word publicly one way or the other. Mr. Wetmore, the candidate with the smallest following, had votes enough, if he could have transferred them to either of his opponents, to insure an election. The session ended in a deadlock. In June Colonel Colt announced his withdrawal from the race. His supporters, like Mr. Wetmore's, being stalwart Republicans, would not vote for Colonel Goddard, because of his affiliation with the Democrats. The issue will be fought out at the polls in October. The adherents of Colonel Goddard hope to capture a majority of the Legislature on joint ballot. They have no chance to get a majority in the State Senate, but they might conceivably obtain a sufficient majority in the House to overcome the Republican Senate majority on joint ballot.

Reformers Control "the Rhode Island Bible"

In the third place, the Providence *Journal*, "the Rhode Island Bible," with its evening edition, the *Bulletin*, has come under the control of men who refuse to sanction or to remain silent upon those corrupt practices that have characterized Republican rule in the State for many years past. One prominent Republican of the faction now opposed by the *Journal* told me, a bit gloomily, that "as goes the *Journal*, so goes Rhode Island." His feelings seemed to be about equally dominated by pride in the *Journal* as an institution and grief for its going astray.

The Metcalfs and other minority stockholders in the *Journal*, believing that its subserviency to ring politicians of the worst sort would finally wreck its influence, united to get control, and brought the paper back into the course where it gained its wealth and power. Under the shrewd and clean editorship of Frederick Roy Martin, a Cambridge and Harvard product, assisted by John R. Rathom, one of the ablest newspaper men the West has produced in many years, as managing editor, the *Journal* is conducting a strong and aggressive campaign for political decency in Rhode Island. Its editors do not join the demand of the more radical Democrats for a convention thoroughly to revise the Constitution of the State. They are sufficiently conservative to urge the taking of one step at a time. The *Journal* does advise amendments giving the Governor the power of veto and granting a larger measure of legislative representation to the cities. Meantime, the *Journal* is supporting the senatorial candidacy of Colonel Goddard, as against Mr. Wetmore or any other man whom the old Republican ring may name. The *Journal*, more than any other factor, drove Colonel Colt out of the race. However others may regard it, this is an achievement upon which the *Journal's* new directors freely felicitate themselves — and Rhode Island.

More than one prominent Republican favored me with his opinion that unless his party shall nominate a candidate known to be proof against bribe-giving, and otherwise of the highest type, the State is pretty certain to choose a legislative majority favorable to the election of Colonel Goddard.

Prospective Constitutional Amendments

Even more important than the men concerned is the movement for two amendments to the State Constitution. Governor Higgins, following the lead of Governors Utter and Garvin, strongly urges an amendment making the Governor a real executive. He believes the Governor of Rhode Island should have the power of veto and the power of appointment which now lodges in the Senate. He told me that his vetoless condition was shared only by the Governor of South Carolina. It is an interesting and perhaps not unsignificant coincidence that Rhode Island and South Carolina, from the beginning of the Union, were most jealous of State's rights and held on longest to the profitable trade in negro slaves.

The second constitutional amendment sought in Rhode Island aims to correct existing inequalities in legislative representation. We have seen how the basis of senatorial representation lodges an overwhelming majority of that body in the hands of a small minority of the people. There are seventy-two members of the lower House, and the number that Providence may elect, irrespective of population, is one-sixth of the whole. When you remember that Providence has five-twelfths of the State's inhabitants you perceive the injustice of that limitation.

There is a feeling in the State, too, that the qualifications for the suffrage ought to be revised. All registered electors can vote for state and national officers, but in city and town elections property qualifications reduce the number of the voters. In the towns this qualification covers real estate, and the would-be voter must hold at least $200 worth of it or he cannot vote on town business. In the cities the voter must have personal property worth $134 in order to vote for city officers. The assessments of these voters are made by a Board of Assessors chosen by the City Council in each instance. Whether true or not, it is commonly charged that the assessors in some of the cities use their power to pack the voting-lists with known supporters of their party. It is said that they frequently neglect to include in the voting-list the names of qualified voters not of their party. The door is obviously open to trickery of this character, and the general tone of Rhode Island politics is not so high as to deprive the charge of all right to consideration.

Masters Versus Workmen

Very naturally, so far as they show any interest in the subject at all, the working people of the State favor manhood suffrage without property qualification of any sort. On the other hand, the masters of the State's politics, the mill millionaires, have a sound reason, from their point of view, for opposing any extension of the suffrage. And they have an equally sound reason, as they see it, for opposing any change in the basis of legislative representation. In the cities, where they are the chief property-owners, they are loath to see any step made that would weaken their control upon the expenditure of money taken in taxes. In the Legislature, they fear nothing else quite as much as hostile labor legislation. While the balance of legislative power remains in the country towns, and is beyond the reach of the working people of the cities, the large manufacturers can reasonably hope to defeat any legislation in the interest of the workers and at the expense of the employers. The President's recommendation of a national employers' liability law that should work automatically, making the employer responsible for his employee's injuries, however caused, would get about one vote out of a hundred if submitted to the manufacturers of Rhode Island for approval. It goes without saying that a Legislature chosen by working men and acting in the interests of the working men as a group, might be expected to enact such a law as the President recommended.

The Secret of Aldrich's Strength

Another possibility which the manufacturers, or most of them, regard with dread is that Rhode Island may, by going Democratic in State elections, give the nation the impression that she desires tariff revision; for Rhode Island is a high-tariff stronghold. Most of the men that have built up her great industries—there are a few exceptions—firmly believe that the success of these industries rests upon the protective-tariff system. A curious illustration of the way they put this factor above all others in considering politics is their attitude toward Senator Aldrich. Republicans, Independents, and Democrats alike assured me that the senator is "the most selfish man that ever drew the breath of life;" that they heartily disapprove his making use of such men as General Brayton to perpetuate himself in office; and that they resent his contemptuous treatment of his constituents, personally.

"Then why," I asked, "do you keep him in office?"

"Because," one man replied, and he voiced the sentiment of the others, "we can't get along without him, dash blank him."

Senator Aldrich, it is said, has been singularly inconsiderate of Rhode Islanders at Washington. This was so much the case that it became the fashion in certain circles to say, "Rhode Island has but one senator — Wetmore." The Newport senator was always studiously careful to respond to every communication from his people, however unimportant — a course in marked contrast with that of his lordly senatorial associate. Notwithstanding this, however, and notwithstanding the well-known fact that Senator Aldrich has been only secondarily Rhode Island's representative, giving his first thought to the great New York financial interests, headed by the Standard Oil Company, whose especial senatorial champion he has been for many years, the business interests of the State have felt that his commanding authority in respect to tariffs made him far the most valuable man the State could send to the Senate. And so they have cursed him for his manners and elected him for his ability, and seem likely to continue doing so for a long time to come, or as long as he wishes to hold office.

Senator Aldrich, like former Governor Odell of New York, was a grocer when he entered politics. But he was something else that Mr. Odell was not; namely, a cold-blooded, iron-willed master of men. He kept on growing past the point where Odell's limitations brought him back to the earth with a dull thud. Mr. Aldrich is credited with having gained a million dollars in the reorganization of the Rhode Island street-railways in 1892. That transaction also laid the foundation for the great fortune of Marsden J. Perry, who, with Mr. Roelker and five other men that could look further ahead than the average, shared the profits of the street-railway reorganization. The deal was a blend of political special favors, watered stock, and ultimate monopoly, but it gave Rhode Island cities a tremendous benefit in a system of street-railway and interurban electric transportation immeasurably superior to that which it replaced; and so possibly the promoters were not extravagantly paid for the brains and energy they put into it.

The men who formed the Rhode Island Company, that monopolized practically all of the trolley-lines of Rhode Island, have since sold out the property to the New York, New Haven & Hartford Railroad. The New Haven is dictator of Connecticut politics, and master at pleasure of Connecticut industry in its relations with transportation.

Reform Movement Not of Popular Origin

An interesting feature of the reform movement in Rhode Island is the fact that it does not originate among the working masses of the people. It seems rather to be a contest between rival groups of millionaires for control of the State's affairs. I suggested to Senator Gardner of Providence that it was a fight between the clean rich and the other sort of rich. He demurred. Mr. Wetmore's supporters, he said, were "clean rich," too. He thought it likely that at least half of them voted for Parker for President in 1904. Against Mr. Wetmore nothing worse has been alleged than that he is a New Yorker, and that he has made liberal contributions to General Brayton's war-bag to insure his election as senator; in short, that he played the game as he found it. If his opponents were defining the position of a man less amiable and friendly than Mr. Wetmore, they would doubtless say flatly that he bought his office. They do not say that, but they arrive at the same conclusion in much gentler terms.

The opponents of Colonel Goddard do not charge that he is trying to buy the senatorship. They admit without question that he would scorn to do anything of that kind. But they do say that the Democratic organization in the State is using him and his presumably liberal campaign contribution for legitimate expenses, as a means of gaining control of the State offices. They do not explain how a Democratic majority in the House could control State appointments that are made by the State Senate, which will certainly remain reliably Republican.

The Senate is "The State"

By the way, here is another curious feature of the Rhode Island political system. The Senate is practically the whole State government. The Governor can nominate men for the various appointive offices under the State government, but in only one or two unimportant instances can he confer such office without the Senate's confirmation. And if the Senate does not wish to confirm, it has only to let three days pass without taking action on the Governor's nominations, when it is free to proceed to make the appointments, without the consent of either Governor or lower House. This is the customary course when the Governor is Democratic. Rhode Island judges, of the Supreme Court and the lower courts, are thus chosen by the Senate, and not, as in most other States, elected by the people. It is not surprising, therefore, to learn that all the members of the present Supreme Court, and all, or nearly all, of the judges of the lower courts, were members of the Legislature when elevated to the bench.

In fact, as matters stand, the people of Rhode Island — the rank and file — have very little control of their State government. The forty votes cast for Colonel Goddard in the senatorial contest represented more than sixty per cent of the voters of the State, but they were far from being a majority of the Legislature.

The Boss and the Governors

Rhode Island politics have brought forward a number of interesting personalities — strongly marked individuals. General Charles R. Brayton, blind giant of sixty-seven years, seated in his office on the top floor of the ten-story Bannigan Building in Providence, alone, received me with a curt refusal to talk — then proceeded to talk in the most entertaining fashion for half an hour. He certainly knows his peculiar business, and he knows human nature. If good men in politics possessed one-half the tact, the courtesy, the genuine human sympathy that make the capital of men of the Brayton sort, the virtue of honesty would be triumphant more often than it is. The successful business man, especially if he be also a scholar, is pretty certain to have lost touch with the common run of humanity, and to fail to understand its instincts. This the successful boss never does. He wins far more men with courtesy than with money, and here is a fact that honorable amateurs in politics seldom comprehend.

The men who are asking Rhode Island to repudiate Brayton and Braytonism, lack something of a complete understanding of the mental processes of the common man, the working man. They call Brayton "Rob Roy," forgetting that Rob Roy was the most popular man in his county, who robbed the rich to share with the poor — popular because his faults were the faults of most men, and linked him to them in a bond of fellowship. The humble bard who wrote of Robert Burns, "We love him for his human faults," put his finger upon one of the most powerful impulses of the human heart.

Governor Higgins, a young lawyer, seems to me a man exceedingly likely to win popular favor. The Governor, like his predecessor, Mr. Utter, is both clean and human. Both men resented General Brayton's presence in the Statehouse. Governor Utter, realizing that he had no authority to force Brayton's withdrawal from the public office where he, a private citizen, sat and ordered the course of legislation, said nothing publicly except in one remarkable platform utterance a few days before the last State election when it was too late to help him or his party.

One morning General Brayton called up the Governor on the telephone and asked him whom he intended to nominate for a certain State office.

"The floor of the Senate, it seems to me, is the place to make that announcement," said Governor Utter, and he hung up the 'phone.

Mr. Utter is a newspaper publisher. His paper, the Westerly *Daily Sun*, is the only daily paper in America that publishes a Sunday evening edition. He is a Seventh Day Baptist. His paper does not appear on Saturday. Westerly is a Seventh Day Baptist stronghold. Many of the stores and professional offices there close on Saturday and are open on Sunday.

Governor Higgins, of a more sanguine temperament than Governor Utter, made a sharper attack upon General Brayton. After trying vainly to induce the blind boss by personal persuasion to leave the capitol, the Governor published an open letter assailing General Brayton in fierce fashion and demanding his withdrawal. High Sheriff White was coupled with Brayton in the Governor's broadside, but both men were obdurate, and the boss held his position in the high sheriff's office until the session closed.

Governor Higgins's Letter to the Sheriff

Governor Higgins's letter deserves a wider reading than it has yet obtained, for its analysis of conditions that prevail in many other State capitols beside that of Rhode Island. The communication, which was addressed to General Hunter C. White, sheriff of Providence County, is as follows:

Sir: On January 26th of this year I had a conference with the State-house commissioners, in which I requested them to instruct you to keep Charles R. Brayton out of your office. They stated to me that they did not believe their power was sufficient under the law to justify them in doing so. They referred me to the Legislature and to you. They suggested that if I called the matter officially to your attention you would probably act.

I have acted in accordance with their suggestion. You will recollect that a few weeks ago I asked you to come to my office, where I privately requested you to remove this disgraceful object from your office. In vain have I appealed to you in private. I now appeal to you publicly. This letter shall be given to the public for the express purpose of calling this matter to the attention of our citizens. I do more than appeal. In the name of the citizens of Rhode Island, I demand that you refuse to allow Boss Brayton to use the property of Rhode Island for his private pleasure and profit. It is a matter of extreme regret to me that the most urgent public necessity impels this request. The wide publicity which has been given Brayton's conduct in this capitol; the impudent manner in which he flaunts himself in the teeth of our people and before the eyes of our legislators; his shameless disregard for the outer forms of public decency, as well as for the elementary rules of proper personal conduct in this building, require that action be taken at once. The people of Rhode Island have tolerated Boss Brayton and his brazen arrogance as long as they should. The time has at last arrived when patience is no longer a virtue, and when in deference to an aroused and indignant sentiment throughout the State this man should be expelled from this capitol.

To none is his conduct better known than to you. Year in and year out he has occupied and used your office for his vile purposes with your knowledge and consent. He could not have appropriated your office without such knowledge and consent. You know that for thirty years this man has been in almost daily attendance upon the sessions of the Legislature, dispensing his orders to certain members with the most imperious despotism. You know that for decades he has stood like an ancient brigand at the door of this capitol and has clubbed into servility and compliance with his demands many seekers of legislation, public and private franchises. You know that for a generation past many citizens have openly charged that it was impossible to secure proper action on certain matters of legislation without first paying tribute to the legislative Rob Roy of these Plantations.

Your office in the Rhode Island State-house (Room 207) has been almost invariably the centre of his activity. Your office, Room 207, has, in other words, been the lobby headquarters of Boss Brayton. The situation, therefore, resolves itself to this: the State-house of Rhode Island, a building paid for by the people of the State, supposed to be used exclusively for public and legitimate purposes, has been turned over, so far as your office has been concerned, to the private and illegitimate use of Boss Brayton.

It cannot truthfully be said that Brayton comes to your office as a private citizen or as a friend. If that were so, why is it that he visits you only on such days and at such times as the Legislature is in session? If he is so extremely solicitous in his friendship for you, why is it that he does not visit you daily at your office in the Providence County court-house? You alone, sir, are picked out as the recipient of a letter of this kind for the reason that you are the only one of all the officials occupying quarters at the State-house who allows those quarters to be used for unlawful lobbying.

I, therefore, again demand of you that this thing cease, and cease at once. I demand that you decline the use of your office to Boss Brayton. This demand is based upon two reasons: first, that neither you nor any other public official has the right to utilize the public property of the State for private or improper purposes. Your room, No. 207, has been assigned to you for the conduct of the duties of your office, not for rent or subletting to those who are in the employ of private corporations or others seeking to secure or prevent legislation. What right has Boss Brayton to Room 207? He holds no public office or commission from the people of this State. What right have you to turn over to him practically the entire possession of that room? Both when you are present and when you are absent the boss is in entire charge and has absolute control of your office. He receives his legislative clients and visitors there; he stations his emissaries at the door of your room, and he, not you, says who shall receive admittance to that room. He acts as if he, not you, were the one to whom that room is assigned. Now I say you have no more right to allow a private individual to take charge of your office and carry on private business, especially private business of a most sordid nature, than I have to use the Governor's office for the conduct of my private law practice. Unless this be so, then every State official who is in any way connected with business enterprises of a public character has full right to transfer his private offices to the Statehouse. Does Brayton pay rent for Room 207 to you or to the State?

The second reason for my demand is that you have no right to encourage a common nuisance on State property. Brayton is unquestionably a common nuisance. You know the man's degenerate character better than I do. You know that he is unfit to hold public office or to be entrusted with any honorable duty. You know that the last federal office he held was surrendered by him in disgrace and by compulsion. You know that he misappropriated the public funds of the United

States while postmaster of the city of Providence. You also know the disgraceful scandals attached to his administration of the office of chief of State police. Yet you daily parade him in the State-house in the eyes of the public as the master of your room there. You know further that it is a matter of common knowledge that Brayton's scandalous lobbying has been practically his only business for the past quarter of a century, and that although nominally a lawyer, he has never engaged in the real practice of the profession, but has been content to acquire a lucrative existence from the fees he has wheedled and whipped out of seekers of legislation and of office.

The boss's continued presence in the capitol offers daily scandal to the men, women, and children of the State. Several times a week children from various parts of the commonwealth come to visit the capitol, and immediately on stepping from the elevator are greeted with this unseemly spectacle in your room. On February 8 nearly two hundred little children from the town of Warwick came to visit the State-house. Many of these children were introduced to Brayton in your office, and shook hands with him. A nice spectacle, is it not, for the youth of the State to witness? A beautiful example, is n't he, for little boys and girls of tender years to gaze upon and look up to with youthful admiration?

In my conference with the State-house commissioners on January 26 it was not denied by them that Brayton was a paid lobbyist and a disgraceful character. One of the commissioners declared that he himself had told you on a former occasion that you ought not to allow the boss to make his headquarters in your office, and that you replied: "What can I do? I would not put Brayton out of my office for all the positions in the State." In other words, you have admitted not only to this commissioner, but to others as well, that you were under obligations of such a nature to the boss that your hands were tied and you would not put him out. Now, sir, I am going to ask you what right you have to barter away the public property and the public honor of this State in the payment of your political obligations? I want to ask you further what right have you to prostitute a public office in this capitol in compensation for the influence of that boss? I want to ask you, further, how long you propose to continue this glaring misconduct? How much longer are you going to fly in the face of public opinion? If you were State Treasurer, do you think you would be justified in taking money from the treasury in order to pay a political debt of yours? If you were the State Librarian, do you think you would be justified in giving away the public books belonging to the State to somebody who helped you to get into office? That, sir, is just what you are now doing, according to your own statement and your own actions. You are turning over to Boss Brayton the public property of the State of Rhode Island (namely, the use of Room 207) because the boss has "made you politically."

It is unnecessary to add that this communication is not prompted by personal ill-feeling or malice toward either you or Boss Brayton. You understand my position thoroughly from the private interview we had a short time ago. I regret further that you force me to the disagreeable task of telling publicly the disgusting story of this man. I had hoped, after our interview, that it would be unnecessary for me openly to refer to the miserable life and character of Charles R. Brayton. I regret, too, that you have not allowed me to look on Brayton as I had wished,—with respect for his war record and pity for his physical infirmity,—rather than with contempt for his thirty years' public infamy. The responsibility, therefore, for this unpleasant task is not on my shoulders. Both you and Brayton have had fair warning. I have tried in every honorable way I knew to avoid resorting to this means, but you would not have it. The gauntlet has been thrown down to me by you both with a spirit of insolent defiance, but I shall not hesitate to pick it up—not in a spirit of pugnacity, but with a firm determination that the right of our people to have their public places kept for proper public uses and free from scandals and nuisances, moral, political, and otherwise, shall be vindicated once and for all.

In the name, therefore, of the decent citizenship of this commonwealth, I demand that you clean this moral and political pest out of your office. In the name of common, civilized virtue, I demand that you no longer persist in allowing a part of this capitol to be used as the headquarters of a notorious lobbyist.

The Reply of the Blind Boss

To which the big blind boss, turning his sightless eyes toward the open window through which he gets a faint lightening of the physical vision, makes answer: "Yes, I know they don't like me; but they know I don't care a damn."

It would be hard to find a more striking contrast than that of the Governor, a slight figure, almost boyish, with his clean, earnest countenance, and the huge gray bulk of the blind boss, alone in his eyrie, his face now as expressionless as a gambler's mask, now breaking into a smile of kindly humor, overlaid with conscious bravado and deeply underlaid with a desolate loneliness of the spirit. Here, as always, youth will be served. The passing of the boss — of this particular boss, at any rate — is already taking place as a part of the general regeneration of Rhode Island's politics.

Except in a few of the country towns, public education in Rhode Island is maintained at a high standard. The statement is made officially that free high-school training is provided for all but five per cent of the children of the State.

As a final word, it may be said that aside from the need to get her boys and girls out of the mills into school, to open up her dusty back-country closets, and to obtain a first-class harbor at Providence, the most pressing business of Rhode Island at this time is to get representative government.

BASIC FACTS

Capital City	Providence
Nickname	Little Rhody
Flower	Violet
Bird	Rhode Island Red
Tree	Red Maple
Song	*Rhode Island*
Rock	Cumberlandite
Entered the Union	May 29, 1790

STATISTICS*

Land Area (square miles)	1,049
Rank in Nation	50th
Population†	969,000
Rank in Nation	39th
Density per square mile	923.7
Number of Representatives in Congress	2
Capital City	Providence
Population	179,116
Rank in State	1st
Largest City	Providence
Population	179,116
Number of Cities and Towns over 10,000 Population‡	25
Number of Counties	5

---

*Based on 1970 census statistics compiled by the Bureau of the Census.
†Estimated by Bureau of the Census for July 1, 1972.
‡Includes 17 towns over 10,000 population.

RHODE ISLAND

MAP OF CONGRESSIONAL DISTRICTS OF RHODE ISLAND

BIOGRAPHICAL DIRECTORY

Arnold, Samuel Greene. <u>History of the State of Rhode Island and Providence Plantations</u>. New York: D. Appleton and Company, 1859-60. 2 vols.

Bates, Frank Greene. <u>Rhode Island and Formation of the Union</u>. New York: Published for Columbia University Press by the Macmillan Company, 1898.

Best, Mary Agnes. <u>The Town that Saved a State</u>. Westerly, R. I.: The Utter Company, 1943.

Bicknell, Thomas Williams. <u>The History of the State of Rhode Island and Providence Plantations</u>. New York: The American Historical Society, Inc. 5 vols.

Carroll, Charles. <u>Rhode Island, Three Centuries of Democracy</u>. New York: Lewis Historical Publishing Company, 1932. 4 vols.

Coleman, Peter J. <u>Transformation of Rhode Island, 1790-1860</u>. Providence: Brown University Press, 1963.

Field, Edward. <u>State of Rhode Island and Providence Plantations</u>. Boston and Syracuse: The Mason Publishing Company, 1902. 3 vols.

Lovejoy, David Sherman. <u>Rhode Island Politics and the American Revolution (1760-1776)</u>. Providence: Brown University Press, 1958.

Polishook, Irwin H. <u>Rhode Island and Union, 1774-1795</u>. Evanston: Northwestern University Press, 1969.

Richman, I. B. <u>Rhode Island: Its Making and Its Meaning</u>. New York and London: G. P. Putnam's Sons, 1902. 2 vols.

Tanner, Earl C. <u>Rhode Island: A Brief History</u>. Providence: Rhode Island State Board of Education, 1954.

Weeden, William Babcock. <u>Early Rhode Island: A Social History of the People</u>. New York: The Grafton Press, 1910.

NAME INDEX

Allen, Philip, 12
Anthony, Henry B., 11
Arnold, Benedict, 3, 4
Arnold, Lemuel H., 10

Ball, Henry, 4
Beeckman, R. Livingston, 15
Benton, William, 3
Block, Adrian, 1
Bourn, Augustus O., 13
Brown, D. Russell, 14
Burnside, Ambrose E., 13

Carr, Caleb, 4
Case, Norman S., 16
Chaffee, John H., 18
Charles II, King of England, 3
Clarke, Walter, 4, 5
Coddington, William, 1, 2
Coddington, William, 3, 4
Coddington, William, 2nd, 4
Coggeshall, John, 2, 4
Cooke, Nicholas, 7
Collins, John, 8
Cozzens, William C., 12
Cranston, John, 4
Cranston, Samuel, 5

Davis, John W., 14
Del Sesto, Christopher, 18
D'Estaing, Count, 7, 8
Dexter, Gregory, 2
Diman, Byran, 11
Dimond, Frances, 12
Dole, Robert,
Dorr, Thomas W., 10, 11
Dyer, Elisha, 12, 15

Easton, John, 4
Easton, Nicholas, 2
Eisenhower, Dwight D., 17
Elizabeth II, Queen of England, 19

Fenner, Arthur, 8
Fenner, James, 9, 11
Flynn, William S., 16
Francis, John B., 10

Garvin, L. F. C., 15
Gibbs, William C., 9
Gorton, Samuel, 1, 2
Green, Nathaniel, 7
Green, Theodore F., 16
Greene, William, 6
Greene, William, 2nd, 8
Gregory, William, 15

Hacklett, Mr., 3
Harris, Elisha, 11
Higgins, James H., 15
Hopkins, Stephen, 6, 7
Hoppin, William W., 12
Howard, Henry, 13
Hutchinson, Anne, 1
Hutchinson, William, 1

Jencks, Joseph, 5
Jones, William, 9

Kimball, Charles Dean, 15
King, Samuel Lee, 11
King, Samuel Ward, 10
Knight, Nehemiah R., 9

Ladd, Herbert W., 14
Licht, Frank, 18, 19
Lippitt, Charles W., 15
Lippitt, Henry, 13
Littlefield, Alfred H., 13
Lyndon, Josias, 7

McGrath, Howard, 17
McKiernan, John S., 17
Mumford, Stephen, 3

Padelford, Seth, 13
Pastore, John O., 17
Pothier, Aram J., 15, 16

Quinn, Robert E., 17

Roberts, Dennis J., 17

Sanford, John, 2
Sanford, Peleg, 4
Sans Souci, Emery J., 16
Slater, Samuel, 8
Smith, Henry, 9
Smith, James Y., 12
Smith, John, 2
Sprague, William, 10, 12
Sullivan, John, 7

Taft, Royal C., 14
Turner, Thomas A., 12

Utter, George H., 15

Vanderbilt, William H., 17
Van Zandt, Charles C., 13
Verrazano, Giovanni da, 1

Wanton, Gideon, 6
Wanton, John, 5
Wanton, Joseph, 7
Wanton, William, 5
Ward, Richard, 6
Ward, Samuel, 6, 7
Washington, George, 5
Wetmore, George P., 14
Wilbur, Isaac, 9
Williams, Roger, 1, 2
Winslow, Josiah, 3
Wolfe, John A., Jr., 18

R01 0846 7793

SR